DRIVING A HARNESS HORSE

A Step-by-Step Guide

The view from the box seat showing the harness fitting comfortably

DRIVING A HARNESS HORSE

A Step-by-Step Guide

SALLIE WALROND L.H.H.I.

A sequel to *Breaking a Horse to Harness*

J. A. Allen
LONDON

By the same author

Fundamentals of Private Driving (The British Driving Society)
A Guide to Driving Horses (Pelham Books)
The Encyclopaedia of Carriage Driving (J.A. Allen)
Looking at Carriages (J.A. Allen)
Breaking a Horse to Harness (J.A. Allen)
Judging Carriage Driving (J.A. Allen)
Handling Your Problem Horse (Swan Hill Press)
Starting to Drive (Kenilworth Press)
Driving Questions Answered (Kenilworth Press)
Driving Dos and Don'ts (Kenilworth Press)

British Library Cataloguing in Publication Data
A catalogue record for this book is available from the British Library

ISBN 978 0 85131 861 5

First Published in 1992 by
J. A. Allen & Co. Ltd.

This edition published in 2002 by J. A. Allen
an imprint of Robert Hale Ltd., Clerkenwell House,
45–47 Clerkenwell Green, London EC1R OHT

www.halebooks.com

Reprinted 2005
Reprinted 2008

Set by Textype, Cambridge
Colour separation by Tenon Polert Colour Scanning Ltd
Printed in Singapore by Kyodo Printing Co (S'pore) Pte Ltd
Designed by Judy Linard

Contents

Acknowledgements

Sallie Walrond would like to thank the following: her husband Bill; Richard James for his valuable advice and additions; Cynthia Haydon, for her help; the late Anne Grahame Johnstone for her line drawings; Carl Barnard, June Hales, Elton Hayes, Julie Hugo, Lara Mockridge, and Araminta Winn for their suggestions for the typescript; Phyllis Candler, Les McCall, Fred and Margaret Collins, Jon and Christine Dick, Peter Durrant, Trina Hall, Heather Kinner, Sidney and Carol Murrell, Michael and Pearl Underwood for their help; and the following for their generous permission to use pictures: Alf Baker (plate 60), Elisabeth Brotherton (56), "Eventer" (63, 71) Jack Field (83), Anne Grimshaw (22, 29, 65, 70), Peter Higby (2, 41), Brian and Chris King (83), Stuart Newsham (58, 82), Tessa Reeve (59), Chris Stross (62), Sally Taylor (61).

The author thanks Patricia Zilli for her help on the day when the photos were shot for this revised and updated edition.

Sallie Walrond also thanks Anthony Reynolds, L.B.I.P.P., L.M.P.A., for the care and attention to detail which he took with the numerous photographs upon which the new edition of this book is based.

Introduction

My earliest memories of driving a harness horse go back to the nineteen forties. I can remember, when I was about nine years old, sitting by the window of the house where I lived in Chiswick, London, waiting for the milkman to arrive with his horse and cart. I had drawn a picture of the horse (whose name I later discovered was Blacky) in his black harness with the white metal fittings. I had memorised the bridle, collar and saddle to my satisfaction, but the mass of straps which made up the breeching were worrying me and I could not get them right. When the horse finally arrived, I could see for myself how it all worked so that I could get my picture finished. It was not long after this that I persuaded this milkman to let me accompany him on the cart. In exchange for delivering milk at a block of flats nearby, where bottles were put into service hatches by the sides of front doors, I was allowed to drive the horse – a black vanner – on the short journey back to the dairy. As far as I was concerned, ten minutes driving was fair exchange for about two hours of delivering milk. Blacky was given his lunch ration of chaff and a few oats in a nosebag strapped onto his head over the bridle, which still included the Wilson snaffle. He stood happily for the period of this lengthy delivery, throwing his nosebag upwards with great expertise, in order to release any oat which had strayed into the leather-bound corner of the cocoa-nut fibre bag. During the winter, a rubber-covered, wool-lined loin sheet was fastened to the saddle to keep his back warm and dry. The cart was a pneumatic-tyred four-wheeler and I used to climb up onto what I thought was a very high seat for the drive back. I made a whip with a stick cut from a tree in Chiswick Park onto which I tied some string, in an effort to make Blacky go faster. It did not have much effect on his rug-covered back, but we seemed to go at quite a speed on this homeward trip.

I spent many hours of the school holidays at the United Dairy Depot. I would stand by the entrance to the long row of stalls, waiting for horses to come back from their day's work. There were thirty or more horses housed in these stables. On returning, the cart would be drawn up alongside the unloading bay. The driver would undo the belly band, breeching and chain-ended traces, in that order. The horse then walked out of the shafts to the water trough where he drank his fill, submerg-

1 *The author, aged about nine years, with Peggy, a vanner, at the United Diary depot in London*

ing his reins and lower parts of the bridle in the process. He then took himself through the door to the row of stalls and walked along until he came to his own stall where he stood and waited for someone to come and take off his harness. Sometimes, a number of horses all came back at the same time; I loved this, as I would then be allowed to unharness one or even two. First the reins were unbuckled and the bridle was removed; next the girth was undone and I pulled everything backwards until the harness all slid off into a heavy heap which I stacked in the passage behind the horse. The collar and hames were usually taken off together and these were too heavy and high for me to reach so had to be left for the grooms. Each horse had a number, by which it was known at the depot, though of course the delivery men all gave their particular horse a name. The number was stamped onto the collar so that no mistakes were made and sore shoulders were avoided. This number was on a metal plate over the horse's stall and it was burned into a front hoof when the animal was shod at the dairy forge.

There were, up until the end of World War Two, a large number of working horses in London. The greengrocer first had a roan cob to draw his four-wheeled cart, and later a fine-legged Hackney pony who pulled so hard that his head was always turned to one side in an effort to restrain his extravagant pace. The coalman and garbage collectors both had heavy, hairy heeled, Shire-type animals with moustaches on their upper lips. The laundry van was pulled by a quality chestnut who appeared to me to go everywhere at a slow canter. I thought that this horse was beautiful – he was always turned out to perfection and his coat gleamed; he wore with pride ribbons and medals of honour, from years of attending London's Van Horse Parade. Another of my favourites was the team of skewbald ponies which pulled a removal van.

The greatest influence on my life came from Dickie and Robert Barley who taught me to ride and drive in Hyde Park. Even at that early age, reins and whip had to be held correctly. Bert was a great coachman. He often put teams of unknown horses together – and they would go well for him. He provided harness horses for a number of businesses and, if a horse had to be taken to replace a sick animal to do the following day's deliveries, I was sometimes allowed to go along. Bert would drive one of the riding school animals which nearly all seemed to go in harness. I would sit beside him in the two-wheeled dog cart and lead the replacement horse as it trotted along behind the cart across London to our destination. On our return, I was occasionally allowed to drive for part of the way and whenever this happened I felt very grand and sat as straight-backed as I could.

One of my first encounters with a set of team harness was when I was told to clean the Road Coach harness, which had brown collars and black pads and bridles. I can remember laying it out on the cobblestones of the Mews yard as though it were on the horses. I had been given strict instructions not to alter any of the buckles into different holes. No doubt, coupling reins had been carefully adjusted in preparation for the following day's work. The Road Coach stood in the yard ready for various commercial activities.

Gradually the working horses were replaced by motorised delivery vans and by the early nineteen fifties there were not many to be seen. A few people drove purely for pleasure but their number was diminishing. The shows at which I competed in the mid fifties with my spotted pony and Skeleton Gig had only two or three entries in the classes for private driving or ride and drive. This pleased me as I then had some chance of winning a red rosette.

Fortunately though, in 1957, a group of carriage-driving enthusiasts led by Mr Sanders Watney realised that unless something constructive were done, the art of carriage driving might become lost for ever. Little had been written on the subject in the early nineteen hundreds because driving was so much a way of life that nothing was being recorded for future generations. A meeting was called and the British Driving Society was formed. It was hoped that perhaps a hundred people might join. The Inaugural Meet and Drive was held at The Royal Windsor Horse Show in May 1958 and fifty-eight members were catalogued. As the British Driving Society grew, Honorary Area Commissioners were appointed to arrange driving meets and activities for members throughout the country, vehicles were unearthed from the backs of barns and harness was discovered in trunks where it had lain untouched for years.

Sandy and Biddy Watney, always generous in their encouragement of young enthusiasts, invited me to visit them on many occasions, so that I could go out with Sandy on his early morning trips with the piebald team and then the greys. He always drove before breakfast in Richmond Park. I learnt a lot from watching the team being harnessed and put to, as well as seeing Sandy's methods of mounting and rein handling. His skill in folding a team whip was noted. I was usually allowed to take the team on an easy bit of road, which was always a thrill. At this time, I was also given the opportunity to drive Sandy's tandem of docked chestnuts, Acrobat and Annabelle, and shown the traditional methods of handling such an equipage.

By the late sixties, the British Driving Society Show was becoming established. It is now the world's largest one-day carriage driving show and more and more shows throughout the country are including driving classes. Horse-driving trials, which began in the early seventies, have developed enormously and there are numerous national events. In 1977, Lady Cromwell and I revived the now flourishing Tandem Club of Great Britain, which had lapsed during the nineteenth century.

Driving clubs are catering for the needs of enthusiasts at local level. Area commissioners all over the country now have assistants in order to cope with the work entailed in the organisation of park and forestry drives, social activities, instructional fixtures and many other functions. Indeed, drivers are now spoiled for choice as dates inevitably clash.

Both the Carriage Association of America and the American Driving Society have large memberships and societies are flourishing in Europe as well as in New Zealand and Australia. This increased interest in what is now generally known as the fastest growing equestrian sport has resulted in a resurgence of skills. Many superb carriages and beautiful sets of harness are being made; as are whips, lamps, coach horns, driving aprons, gloves and numerous other items. More horses and ponies are being broken to harness and the demand for knowledge is increasing. It is now very important that the present generation of carriage drivers should continue to practise the traditional methods which have been proved, for centuries, to be the safest and most efficient way of driving a harness horse.

How to start

The newcomer to carriage driving is often so bewildered by the variety of horses, carriages and harness which is available, that he or she does not know where or how to begin. The best and usually the cheapest way to start is by having a few lessons with an established expert in the art of carriage driving. Names and addresses can be obtained from the British Driving Society in the UK and from secretaries of driving societies around the world, who, in turn, will know of local activities of interest. It is also a good idea to spend some time attending various driving shows, events and meets. The newcomer will be able to learn a lot by looking at the types of horses, carriages and harness which people are using. An enormous amount can be seen by wandering around the horse-box parking area. Driving people are generally found to be friendly and helpful, and ideas can be picked up along with differing points of view. It is important, however, not to burden competitors with questions when they are quite clearly getting ready to compete; nothing is more infuriating. There is so much to think about at this stage that questions from strangers are unlikely to be well received and replies may, understandably, be short.

At large shows and events, there are frequently trade stands with carriages, harness, whips, lamps and numerous driving-related items for sale, and it is useful to look at what is on offer within the various price ranges. Remember that it is often quite easy to buy but not always easy to sell items which are misfits or of poor quality. So, until some knowledge has been gained, it is advisable only to look and compare.

The horse

It is generally unwise to purchase a vehicle or harness before buying the horse. Finding a suitable animal may be difficult; having to obtain one which fits a specific carriage or set of harness only adds to the problem.

The dictum 'buyer beware' is never more true than when selecting a suitable driving animal. Accounts such as: 'we believe that he was driven by his last owner' could mean that he was once put to, having been incorrectly or carelessly harnessed, so that he took off and kicked his way out of the vehicle. Such an animal is unlikely to forget the drama and will probably never be one hundred per cent safe to drive. The comment: 'he has not seen much traffic as we live in a quiet part' could really mean: 'will not face any traffic at all'. Also to be treated with caution are such excuses as: 'we no longer have a vehicle so you can't see him driven' and: 'we can't get the blacksmith so you can't see him on the road'. A hogged mane could mean that the horse suffers from sweet itch, and a very thin animal with misshapen feet might be one which cannot be given grass because this immediately brings on laminitis.

There is a great deal to be said for training the children's outgrown, much loved, pony. Such an animal is likely to have been so accustomed to all manner of games that he is quite likely to take to the idea of pulling a cart without too much trouble. If the owners are experienced horsemen, then there is no reason why they should not train this animal themselves. If they are not very experienced, then it is probably wiser to send the pony to a knowledgeable horse trainer for this specialised job.

Another very good way of getting a suitable driving horse is to buy a foal, yearling or unbroken but well-handled two-year-old, and train the animal to the desired finished product over several years. This, undoubtedly, is the most rewarding way of getting what is wanted. However, not everyone is prepared to wait for several years or to put in the tremendous amount of work entailed. Also, it is not really a good idea for a novice Whip to try to produce a youngster, as this would be a case of the blind leading the blind. A step-by-step guide to the author's well tried and tested method of training is described in *Breaking a Horse to Harness*.

2 *The author driving her Connemara pony, Watchover Cocktail, to a Skeleton Gig to win a Concours d'Elegance class.*

It is, of course, sometimes possible to find a driving horse which is genuine and experienced, but it may take a long time and a lot of searching. Animals may be sold for domestic reasons or because of a change of direction in which the owner is going in competition. So, not all which are offered for sale are rogues. If the beginner to driving is an experienced horseman, then the problem of finding a suitable animal is greatly lessened. He will be able to cope with minor problems as he will be likely to have dealt with them, with a riding horse, in the past. Should a young horse be chosen, then the breed and type of animal will probably depend on the purpose for which he is going to be used. In general, native ponies take quite readily to

17

being trained for harness. The breed chosen often depends on local availability – breeds such as Highlands are popular in Scotland, and Dales and Fells in the north of England; Connemaras are seen in great numbers in Ireland and the author favours them for their type and equable temperament; Welsh ponies and cobs are popular everywhere, as are Shetlands; Dartmoors and Exmoors have their place, as do Norwegian Fjords and Haflingers. Many of these ponies and crosses within the breeds have excellent temperaments which make them suitable for driving. The Hackney, which is the true harness horse, is more suitable for an experienced driver – who will be capable of producing spectacular results from such an animal. Horses which are either pure or part Arab or Thoroughbred are often inclined to be more difficult for a novice to drive. Their greater sensitivity results in less tolerance to the uncomfortable situations which a beginner may unwittingly cause. Such horses as Cleveland Bays, Gelderlanders and those from Hungary, Sweden, Austria and Germany are sought for work in pairs and teams where they look magnificent. Also popular are Morgan Horses from America and Friesians from Holland. The breeds and types from which to choose are almost endless. The person who has never ridden or even handled horses before, but decided to take up driving, is the most vulnerable when it comes to buying a suitable animal. The best thing such an enthusiast can do, after finding a horse which he likes, is to ask the advice of a qualified driving instructor before finalising the deal. Once the animal has been driven and approved by this expert, it can be vetted and then purchased.

It is wise to take the animal straight to the expert's stables so that daily instruction in all aspects of the care of the horse, as well as the driving, can be absorbed. A routine of management will be learned and established. The horse will be harnessed, put to and driven under supervision during these important formative days; incorrect fitting of harness will be avoided. Mistakes in putting to, which could prove disastrous, will not be made: driving will be a pleasure instead of a worry. Any minor problems which, in the hands of a novice, can become major, will be dealt with as they occur and accidents will be prevented. Once confidence is gained and a bond begins to build up between the animal and his new owner, the horse can be taken to his new home. Again, it is advisable for the expert instructor to accompany his pupil on the first occasion that the horse is driven, to check that all goes well in the new surroundings.

It is sensible to budget for the inclusion of the cost of all this help in the price of buying the new horse. The money will be well spent: it could easily save the expense of a smashed-up vehicle, broken harness and a horse which is ruined for life. Before driving on public highways, it is essential to take out adequate third-party insurance cover. Failure to do so is to risk a claim which could result in bankruptcy.

The harness

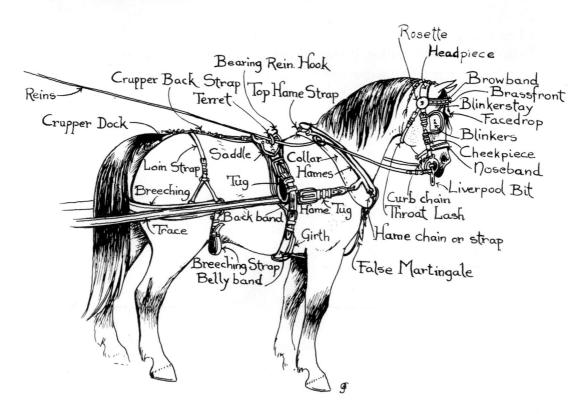

Fig 1. *Parts of harness*

A lot of new harness is made from webbing, nylon and various man-made materials. This is favoured by many people because it is very strong and needs little maintainance. Some can even be put into a bag and placed in the washing machine when it needs to be cleaned. The disadvantage of some of these sets is that they are unlikely to break. If the horse is wearing virtually unbreakable harness and put to a metal vehicle then there is only one thing left to break in a serious incident, and that is the horse. Harness of this kind is, however, widely used by a great number of competitors in driving trials with enormous success. It is useful for everyday exercising as very little time needs to be spent in cleaning.

The author prefers everyday harness which is made of buffalo hide, canvas and felt. It is soft to handle and the buckles can be altered easily, using different holes as required. It needs little attention apart from drying the felt after use and feeding the leather regularly with Ko-cho-line or saddle soap. It has brass fittings which can be polished when time permits.

Brown or black leather harness, built to a traditional pattern, is practical for everyday use but needs more care and attention to keep it in good condition. It can be highly polished if desired, and will look extremely smart. In fact, high-quality, polished, brown harness is just as suitable for showing as black-patent harness providing that it is used with a varnished vehicle. It is not correct to use brown harness with a painted vehicle.

A set of patent-trimmed harness is generally used for most showing classes. This is correct with either a painted or a varnished vehicle. Such a set of harness is not made entirely from patent leather because parts of this would crack and not look smart for very long. The bridle has patent leather on the outer sides of the blinkers; it sometimes has patent on the brow band, behind the brass front which is put on for decoration. The author uses a rolled patent leather brow band, nose-band front and throatlash on her show harness, which looks very smart. The collar of this harness is covered with patent leather and has a plain lining so that it can be kept soft. The hame straps are of plain leather. The saddle is covered with patent leather and has plain leather for the lining, girth straps and girth. The belly band, tugs, back band and all the straps which make up the crupper and breeching are of plain leather so that they can be kept soft and will not crack where they bend. The reins are of brown leather, sometimes called 'London tan', because black leather would leave dye on the gloves in particular, and the clothes in general. Some people have reins which are made of black leather from the rein billet to the splice, which is where the reins are joined at about halfway, and brown leather where they then come back to the driver's hands.

Most show quality harness has brass fittings, called furniture, as brass is now generally preferred. Often, in days gone by, the deciding factor as to whether the fittings should be of brass or white metal was related to one of the family's colours in the coat of arms. Metal was used throughout the harness, carriage, coachman's and footman's livery buttons, to match that on the harness. Possibly it is because white metal was often employed by tradesmen for their harness, as it did not have to be cleaned, that brass furniture has now become so popular for private driving. (The term 'private driving' is used to differentiate driving for pleasure from driving for commercial purposes.) Some show harness in Australia is furnished with gold-plated fittings.

There are quite a number of craftsmen who will make a set of harness specifically to suit the requirements of the purchaser. This entails many hours of highly skilled work and so is, understandably, expensive. However, it must be remembered that such a set will, if cared for, last for well over a lifetime and will bring endless joy to its owner. Names of harness makers can be obtained from secretaries of driving societies.

If the newcomer decides to get second-hand harness, it is very important to take every piece apart and inspect it for wear. If there is the slightest doubt about any part, it is safest to get it renewed by a craftsman. Particular attention must be paid to the reins, bridle billets (points of leather which go round the bit), cheek pieces, hame straps and back band, though *every* part is important. Beware of purchasing a second-hand set which is too expensive in relation to the amount of repairs which need to be done. On the other hand, if it is possible to buy a very old high quality set cheaply, then all the parts such as the blinkers, saddle, collar and brass furniture could be used as a basis for a beautiful new set. The cost may not be much less than entirely new harness but the end result is likely to be superb if the work is carried out by a skilled craftsman. Brass buckles which have been repeatedly cleaned over a great many years have all the little pits polished out and reflect the light better than many of the new brass fittings which are now on sale.

Assembling the harness

The breast collar

A breast collar consists of the padded part which goes round the horse's chest and the neck strap which holds it up in the correct position. The neck strap is usually attached by points which go into small buckles on straps fixed to the breast part. At each end of the breast strap is a large buckle, with a steel tongue, onto which the traces are fixed. It is by these that the draught is transmitted from the horse's shoulders down to the trace hooks on either end of the swingle tree at the front of the vehicle.

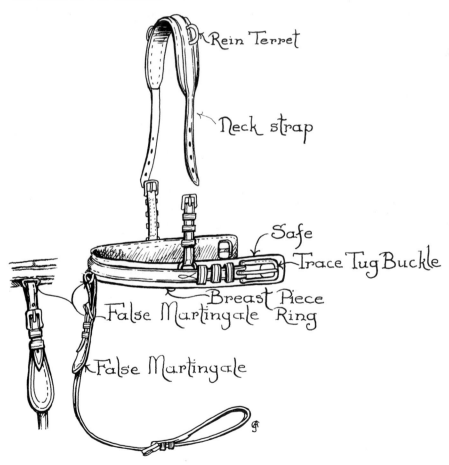

Fig 2. *Parts of a breast collar*
False martingale

False martingale

Some harness has a false martingale. There is a point and buckle at one end which is fixed to a lower dee on the centre of the breast part of a breast collar or to the bottom of a full collar. There is a loop at the other end through which the girth and belly band pass.

Full collar and hames for single harness

The hames are fixed to the collar by a hame strap at the top and either a hame chain or a hame strap at the bottom depending on the design of the hames. Whether the hames are fixed to the collar before it is put on the horse or whether they are put on separately will depend on the conformation or stage of training of the animal. If the horse has a wide forehead and perhaps a thin or narrow neck, then the collar which fits correctly and comfortably on the shoulders will perhaps be too narrow, once the hames are strapped in place, to put over the eyes. When the hames are attached, the collar is narrowed slightly. This can make it impossible to get it over the eyes. Also, if the horse is young or nervous of having the collar with the hames attached put over his head,

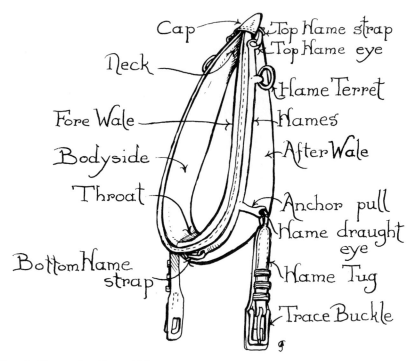

Fig. 3 *Parts of collar and hames*

24

difficulties can be created and a problem developed. In any case, whichever method of harnessing is applied, the hame straps are still put onto the hames in readiness. The hame straps should be tightened from the nearside so each hame strap is initially fastened to the offside hame. The point of the hame strap is passed through the eye of the hame from the outside and then brought back through the underneath keeper and pulled through until the strap is held securely in place on the eye of the offside hame with the buckle on the outer side. The top hame strap is left like this in readiness for when the hames are put onto the collar. The lower hame strap is attached, in this way, and then buckled onto the nearside hame to join the two hames together. If a hame chain is used at the bottom then this serves the same purpose.

Split collars are made specifically to open as they are put over the neck and are used in the case of an extremely narrow neck in comparison with the width of the forehead. The opening at the top enables the collar to be slipped over the neck. The top is then buckled together before the hames are put on and strapped into place. Generally speaking, a split collar does not sit as neatly on the neck as an ordinary full collar which is made in a complete oval. Split collars are frequently favoured for use with donkeys.

The saddle, crupper and full breeching

The saddle, referred to as the pad with pair harness, crupper and breeching and all that go with it can consist of as many as fifteen pieces: the saddle, two terrets, back band, two tugs, girth, belly band, crupper back strap, loose keeper, crupper dock, loin strap, seat of breeching and two breeching straps. The parts vary slightly, according to the design of the harness, but their functions are similar.

If the harness is made of leather to a traditional pattern, the back band is put through a slot in the top of the saddle which will be seen to run across the tree and on top of the padding. Harness of modern design may be found to have loops on top of the saddle to take the back band. This can apply equally to harness made of webbing or buffalo hide and canvas. Some harness is made with the back band fixed to the saddle. This is not satisfactory and can be dangerous because there is a tendency for the saddle to get pulled sideways by the shafts. This is particularly likely to happen if the vehicle is being driven along a sideways sloping track and it can give the horse a sore back. Worst of

25

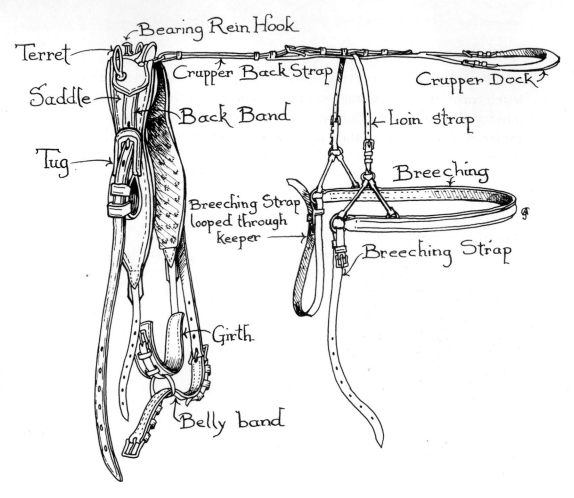

Terret

Saddle

Tug

Bearing Rein Hook

Crupper Back Strap

Back Band

Breeching Strap
looped through
Keeper

Girth.

Belly band

Crupper Dock

Loin strap

Breeching

Breeching Strap

Fig. 4 *Saddle, crupper and breeching*

all are saddles which appear to be made of leather to the traditional design, but on closer inspection it is found that the back band is made in two separate pieces and does not pass over the top of the horse's back. Each side is held in position by the rein terret which goes down through the saddle and lies in a hole punched in the back band piece. This is very dangerous because of the possibility of the leather tearing if strain is put onto the back band if, for some reason, the carriage becomes shaft heavy. If the back band were to break, the shafts would then fall to the ground and there would almost certainly be a horrible accident. The importance of the need for strength in the back band is why this part of the harness is traditionally made with two layers of leather, like the traces. In fact, at first glance, a beginner can find it confusing to differentiate between the traces and the back band. The back band has holes on each side of the centre, to take the shaft tugs, and holes at each end for the belly band. The traces only have holes at one end to fasten them to the hame tugs and one or two large crew holes at the other end to go onto the trace hooks on the vehicle. Next, the terrets are screwed into place in their slots on the top of the saddle. If these terrets are put in before the back band is pushed through the slot, it may be found impossible to get the back band to run through. When the terrets are screwed in, they should not be forced down too tightly because this can dent the leather or stop the back band from moving through the saddle. They should just be secure enough so that they do not move when the reins are put through. Some modern harness has rings or dees which are sewn permanently in place to form terrets. If there is a central bearing rein hook, this is always secured with a bolt, or similar fixing, in the saddle and does not come out. Each tug can now be put onto one of the uppermost sets of holes of the back band so that each lies around the centre of the swell of the saddle to take the shafts. High-quality harness will be found to have a safe behind the tug buckle. This is a piece of leather, or two layers of leather stitched together, with a hole through which the back band passes as well as going through the buckle. Pressure from the tug buckle is taken on the safe and therefore any wear which would otherwise be put onto the back band is transferred to the safe.

The belly band can now be buckled onto the offside into one of the holes of the lower end of the back band. The nearside is left undone in preparation for putting the harness onto the horse. The girth is put onto the offside girth point of the saddle. Again, the nearside is left unbuckled so that the saddle can be put onto the horse. The crupper back strap comes next. There is a little loose keeper which has a habit of getting lost (second-hand harness will frequently come without it); this is threaded onto the crupper back strap. The point of the back strap is put through the dee at the back of the saddle from the underneath upwards and then taken back through the keeper which holds the back strap together, before being buckled. Some cruppers have the dock part sewn onto the back strap and others are fixed with one or two buckles. Whichever is the case, the dock, which may, with high-quality harness, be found to be filled with actual lin-seeds to keep it soft, is fastened to the crupper back strap.

The breeching is now put on. First, the loin strap is threaded through a slot in the crupper back strap. Very often, there is a choice of two or three slots and it will be found that one in particular will provide the best position to enable the breeching to lie correctly. Some loin straps consist of a single strap whilst others branch out into two points with holes to allow for more adjustment when the time comes to put the horse to the vehicle. Whatever the method, the seat of the breeching can now be buckled on each side, to the loin strap. The design of the breeching seat is similar, in many ways, to that of a breast collar and can be confusing to a beginner as they are both padded and often stitched in the same way. One obvious difference is that whereas a breast collar has a buckle at either end, to take the traces, the breeching has large rings to take the breeching straps. These are put onto the breeching seat and each will be found to have a keeper on one side and one or two keepers on the other. The point of the breeching strap is passed through the ring at the end of the seat, with the buckle on the outer side. The point is then passed through the single keeper and pulled right through until the buckle is lying right up by the ring and the strap is fixed, securely in position. False breeching (sometimes called Dr Brown's breeching) can be used instead of full breeching. It consists of a padded breeching seat which is attached to the vehicle, not the horse, by two straps going through specially designed fittings at the ends of the breeching, before they are taken through dees on the shafts.

Fig. 5 *False breeching*

Tilbury tugs

If the harness is to be used with a four-wheeled vehicle, then Tilbury tugs may be employed instead of open tugs in order to keep the shafts steady. The parts which make up a Tilbury tug consist of a shorter back band than is used with ordinary, open, shaft tugs. It is made to the same strength as a normal back band and passes through the slot in the top of the saddle in the same way, although there is very little weight to be taken on the horse's back with a four-wheeler. Tilbury tugs were originally designed to be used with Tilbury gigs which, of course, were two-wheeled. It is probably for this reason that they are still made to the same strength. The back band is shorter because it only has to reach as far as the tug buckles on each side. After the tug is buckled, the points of the back band are passed through the bottom of the buckles on each side. The Tilbury tugs have metal loops on the outer sides of the lower end of the tug buckles. These are covered with leather and it is on these that each shaft rests. There is a point strap sewn to the outer side of the loop which is passed over the shaft to hold it in place. The point strap is buckled to the belly band which, because it is fastened tighter than the usual belly band, is shorter.

Fig. 6 *Tilbury tug*

The bridle

A driving bridle can cause a problem when a beginner first comes to put it together. In fact, it is not as difficult as it appears. It is simplest to take one rosette and slide the dee, at the back, over the end of the brow band and leave it halfway along the loop. Next, take the head piece and put one point through one side of the rosette dee where it is lying over the loop of the brow band and the second point on the other side of the rosette dee and through the other side of the same loop on the brow band. It will now be found that the brow band, head piece and rosette are held in position and the brow band cannot rise upwards, which is the reason for the rosette being used. Its purpose is to prevent the brow band going up and allowing the horse to see backwards behind his blinkers. When putting the brow band onto the head piece be certain that the centre blinker stay buckle is facing in the same direction as the brow band. Take the second rosette and repeat the process so that the brow band is now attached to the head piece. Next, take the cheek pieces which have the blinkers and blinker stays. Buckle the point on the blinker stays to the buckle on the centre of the head piece passing them under the brow band. Now, making sure that there are no twists in the blinker stays, fasten the top buckles above the blinkers to the

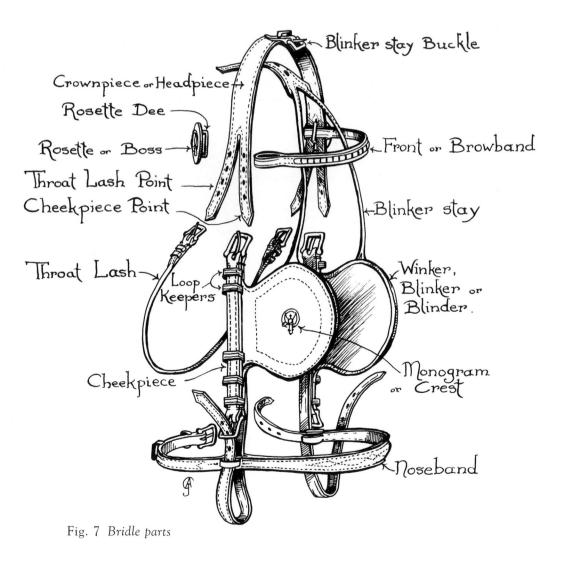

Fig. 7 *Bridle parts*

head piece on each side below the rosettes. The height of the blinkers is adjusted at these buckles.

The noseband is put on next. Be careful to put it on the right way round. For a single horse, it should fasten on the nearside so the buckle end will lie on the offside and the point end will lie on the nearside. Take the cheek-piece point, below the blinkers, and pass it down through the slot in the noseband. This point is now put through the eye at the top of the bit, in the case of a curb bit like a Liverpool, or the floating ring in the case of a Wilson snaffle, and brought up through the keeper on the outer side of the noseband before being buckled below the blinker. This is repeated on the other side. The height of the bit is adjusted at these buckles.

The throatlash is buckled onto the offside point of the head piece and left unbuckled on the nearside in preparation for putting the bridle onto the horse. Some throatlashes have oval or round-shaped rings below the buckle. These are bearing-rein drops and are quite acceptable even if a bearing rein is not worn.

Some bridles have a face drop. This is an oval-shaped piece of leather which is buckled to the centre of the head piece to lie on the forehead between the blinker stays. It is mainly for decoration and can cause irritation to some horses.

Care of the harness

A set of harness needs feeding and looking after with the same attention to detail that is paid to the horse. Harness should not be put away uncleaned if it has got wet or muddy. The leather will almost certainly crack and will eventually harden so much that it may break. If it is kept soft and pliable, breakages are much less likely to occur. The most vulnerable parts of the leather are the parts which come into contact with metal, sweat or saliva. There is no point in cleaning a set of harness without first taking it apart. The areas of leather which are behind buckles are where damp is retained and cracks develop. It is here where breaks often occur when strain is applied.

To clean the harness every buckle must be undone and every part must be separated. A set of single harness will take apart into about thirty-five pieces. It is important to wipe all sweat, grease and mud from the leather before any saddle soap or softener is applied. Excessive water must not be used, neither must the water be too hot. On no account must leather be put into a bucket of water to remove dirt as this will do considerable harm. A cloth which has been put into warm water and then wrung out thoroughly should be used for removing the dirt. Saddle soap is usually best for keeping the leather soft. It should be well rubbed into all the surfaces. Particular attention needs to be paid to any places where the leather comes into contact with metal. The rein billets and bridle cheek pieces, which take most pressure from the bit, can be very vulnerable areas and need a lot of feeding. Outer surfaces of such parts as the back band, traces, breeching seat and breast collar can later be polished to give a shine. It is, though, more important to keep them fed and soft than to get a shine.

Some plain leather harness can look superb, with a mirror-like glow, but be quite dangerous because in the desire to get a shine, the need to keep it soft has been neglected. This usually results in breakages and perhaps an accident. It is quite possible both to soften and polish the leather though it takes a lot more time and effort. Patent leather, on show harness, is best cleaned with special patent cleaner. Very often, a rub with a soft cloth is all that is necessary on patent covered areas.

If leather harness has become very wet, it should be cleaned as just described and left apart, in a reasonably warm atmosphere, to dry thoroughly before being assembled again. It must not be put too near to a boiler as this will cause the leather to dry too quickly and result in cracks. Once it has dried and the water has evaporated, it will be found that the initial application of saddle soap will have disappeared without trace. It will look as though none was ever applied. The leather is likely to feel hard and look dry. It is necessary to give this leather another feed before it is used on the horse. A cleaner called Hide Food is excellent for such occasions, as is another called Ko-cho-line. Whichever is used, the system is to take a little on the hand and to rub it into the inner surface of all the leather parts until it disappears. The result is very satisfying as the leather softens immediately and feels supple again. It is probably because leather harness needs such a lot of care and attention, that many people use webbing and nylon harness.

Any harness which has felt linings to such areas as the breast collar, saddle or breeching seat needs to be dried after use if it has got wet from sweat or rain. It should then be brushed to keep it soft and free from abrasive grit or dried sweat, which could cause sore shoulders, backs or hindquarters. Brass or white metal furniture, on any harness, needs careful cleaning. Metal cleaner must not come into contact with leather because it will harm the hide and will also dry white and ruin the look of the harness. Particular care has to be taken when cleaning any metal areas, like brow band fronts, which have leather backings. It is easy for these to get filled with metal polish. Once this has happened it is almost impossible to remove the dried cleaner from the recesses.

Once all the metal parts have been cleaned, the harness can be put together again and hung up on harness racks which allow circulation of air. The ravages of woodworm, moths and mice should be watched for, since a great deal of harm can be done in quite a short time to a set of harness which is left at the back of a little-used damp cupboard. Harness can rot if it is bundled into a plastic bag where condensation builds up and corrosion develops. If harness is being put away for the winter, it should not be left assembled but should be stored with the buckles undone. In general, points of leather can be passed through keepers, instead of buckles, to avoid metal lying against leather. A whole set can be hung up on harness racks in this way. The bit should remain off the bridle. If harness is not being used for some time it is quite a good idea to take this opportunity to put a little Ko-cho-line into every part where the leather bends round a buckle at the buckle

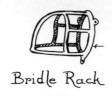

Bridle Rack

Saddle Rack

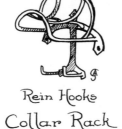

Rein Hooks
Collar Rack

Fig. 8 *Harness racks*

tongue slot. This will soak in gradually and prevent breakages in this vulnerable area.

If the harness is being cleaned before a show, it needs to be assembled and packed carefully ready for travelling. A large suitcase is usually big enough to hold a set of single harness. One way of packing is to put an old towel on the base of the case and the collar, without the hames, can be covered with the towel. The saddle comes next. An old pair of pyjamas works well to protect the polish or patent. Each side of the saddle is placed in a leg, the top of the saddle and shiny terrets are wrapped in the seat of the pyjamas, the back band, tugs and belly band all lie on the outer side of the leg of material. The crupper and breeching fit into the centre of the saddle on top of the collar. Reins also fit in the centre. The hames and traces can now be wrapped and laid carefully in any available space. It is quite a good idea to have some felt covers for the blinkers, to prevent them from getting scratched. The bridle can be put into a pillowcase and placed on top. The whole is covered with more towels and should keep clean and ready to put onto the horse.

If for any reason any part of the harness has been left off the set, it is a good idea to put a note on the lid as a reminder. So often, a cry of dismay is heard in the horse-box area, from someone who has left a vital piece of harness at home on the kitchen table. If the atmosphere is likely to be damp, the metal parts can be covered with cling film to protect them from tarnishing after the harness has been cleaned. The disadvantage of this is that it takes quite a long time to remove it at the show, before harnessing the horse, so time must be allowed.

Harnessing the horse

Putting on a full collar

When harnessing, the collar, whether it is full or breast, is always put on first. This has become a tradition and many people, including the author (who is not normally superstitious), will not drive a horse which has been harnessed in any other way, for fear of an accident. The original reason for the collar being put on first is that in the days of coaching and working horses, the collar, hames, traces and false martingale were frequently put onto the horse as a single unit. Then, when the pad or saddle was put on, the loop of the false martingale was taken up in the girth before the girth was buckled at the girth point. Had the saddle been put on before the collar and martingale, the girth would have had to be unbuckled to take up the martingale. It was to save time and effort that the collar was always put on before the pad or saddle.

It is safer when handling an unknown horse, or a new collar, to put the collar over the animal's head without the hames. Once it is discovered that the collar, hames and traces can easily be passed over the head in one unit, then this can be preferable as it saves a lot of time. But, if in any doubt, put them on independently. Before putting the collar over the horse's head, it is sometimes necessary to stretch it widthways to

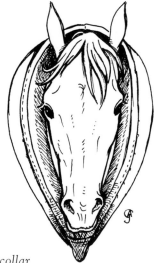

Fig. 9 *How to put on a collar*

35

3 Putting on a collar. A rope halter is being used, in preference to a head collar, because of the danger of the point of the head collar buckle damaging the lining of the collar.

4 The collar, upside down, in readiness for putting on the hames.

5 *The hames buckled in place in the groove of the collar.*

6 *The collar is turned.*

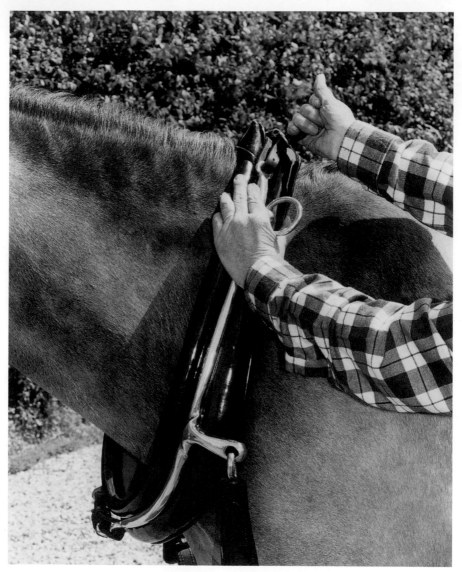

7 *The hame strap is tightened.*

widen it by about half an inch. This must be done very gently in order not to damage the structure of the collar. Some horses can become shy if the collar is forced over the sensitive skin above their eyes. The collar is put on upside down which enables the widest part to pass over the broadest point of the head. Some experienced horses will shut their eyes and push their heads into the collar when they are being harnessed. If the hames are put on separately, it is easier to leave the

8 *The false martingale buckled round the collar and hame strap.*

collar upside down on the animal's neck until the hames have been put in place. The hames are then laid into the groove and held together by the bottom hame strap or chain. The top hame strap, which is at the bottom of the neck at this stage, is buckled tightly enough to secure the hames in place on the collar.

The collar is now put up near the throat, at the narrowest part of the horse's neck, and turned round in the direction in which the mane lies. It is then slid down the horse's neck until it rests against the shoulders and the top hame strap is tightened from the nearside.

The false martingale is buckled round the collar and hames in order to keep the collar down, particularly in the case of a single horse turn-out where the animal may have an extravagant action which could cause the collar to be tilted upwards. False martingales are always worn with pairs and team wheelers, owing to the pressure from the pole straps on the bottom of the hames through the kidney link ring. This gives further reason for the tradition concerning the order of harnessing the horse because, for coaching, false martingales were always worn. The fit of a full collar is extremely important. One which does not fit is certain to result in sore shoulders and an animal having to be laid off his work in harness.

A collar must fit the horse as well as a pair of shoes should fit his owner. One which is too large, small, tight or loose will chafe in exactly the same way that ill-fitting shoes can hurt a human. Sore shoulders, to a horse, can most easily be compared with blistered feet caused by walking too far in ill-fitting shoes. If the collar is not deep enough, pressure will be put onto the windpipe causing a lot of suffering to the horse when he tries to pull the vehicle; this is known as 'piping' the horse. A collar which is too deep will rise upwards and a triangle of light will be seen above the horse's neck when he gets into draught. If the collar is too narrow, it will pinch the neck. Too wide a collar will rock from side to side and chafe the neck and shoulders. There should be enough room at the bottom of the collar to allow the hand to pass freely between the windpipe and the collar. There should just be space for the flat of a narrow hand to lie between the collar and the side of the neck. If there is too much space the collar will rock. When the collar is seen from the rear, it should lie firmly against the horse's shoulders and daylight must not be seen between the collar and the horse. It is quite usual for a collar which fitted in the autumn to be too tight or too loose the following spring, depending on whether the horse has gained or lost condition during the winter months.

Measuring a horse for a collar can be very difficult. The best way is to try a variety of collars and measure the one which fits the best. Then a template can be drawn on a large sheet of paper and measurements taken from that. The collar is measured from the top to the bottom, on the inside where the forewale joins the lining and across the widest part at the bottom end. A likely measurement for a 14.2 hand Connemara type of pony might be fifty-three centimetres (twenty-one inches) deep by twenty-three centimetres (nine inches) across. Once a template is drawn, it can then be carried to such places as auctions and any available collars can be laid onto the paper and compared for size. If a suitable collar is found, even if

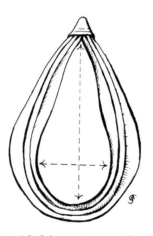

Fig. 10 *Measuring a collar*

straw is sticking out if its sides, it can be restored by a harness or collar maker. The outward appearance is therefore less important than the size and shape, providing that the cost is not too great. Very often, an old collar which has been correctly made, with the straw carefully packed, is preferable – once it is recovered and relined – to a modern collar which may not be as skilfully made. Collar making is an art which is not practised by many people. The most flattering shaped collar for a show animal to wear is one which is swept back, as this shows the animal's neck to greatest advantage. Comparisons can be made by seeing the same pony wearing a swept-back showing collar and a straight, rather heavy, working collar: one is flattering and the other is unflattering.

9 A swept-back collar, which is too deep for this pony.

10 A straight collar, which fits comfortably.

Putting on the breast collar

There are various ways of putting a breast collar and traces onto the horse. One is by unbuckling the neck strap and placing the breast collar round the neck before rebuckling. Another is to hold the breast collar upside down and pass it over the head. This will be found to be easier than placing it over the head the correct way up as the weight of the breast part makes this more difficult. Some people prefer to buckle the traces onto the collar after it has been put onto the horse. If a false martingale is used, this is buckled onto the centre dee at the front of the breast part.

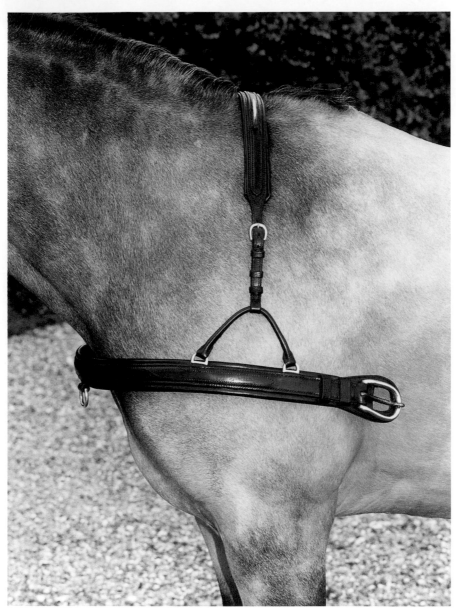

11 *A breast collar.*

The advantage of a breast collar, as opposed to a full collar, is that it can be adjusted to fit a variety of different animals within a certain size limit. Once the breast collar is in place it is then adjusted to fit comfortably. It is essential that the breast part lies on the area below the windpipe and above the point of the shoulder. Pressure on the windpipe will almost certainly cause great discomfort and result in the animal stopping. Equally, chafing below the point of the shoulder will cause distress and prevent the horse from being able to work correctly.

It is essential to use a swingle tree on the vehicle when a breast collar is employed. If a breast collar is used with fixed trace hooks the horse will almost certainly get sore shoulders. As the horse trots, so the breast collar is pulled from side to side by the unyielding, fixed hooks. It will not be long before this constant friction leads to sore shoulders and the animal will then associate pulling with pain. Reaction to this can emerge in many different ways. Some animals will refuse to move forward. If forced by means of a whip, the horse may leap forward into his collar with a series of plunges and rears. Extreme cases may lie down. Once an animal has thrown itself down and has discovered the effectiveness of this means of resistance, a repetition is likely whenever the going gets tough; a horse with this vice is unfit for harness work.

Evidence of sore shoulders is easy to recognise. The horse will quite likely appear to have worked happily. On being unharnessed, patches of

12 A swingle tree.

sweat may be seen on areas where the harness has been, such as the shoulders, under the saddle and behind the ears. If, later in the day, when the horse is put to bed, it is noticed that all the patches which were sweaty have dried, apart from a couple of tell-tale areas where the collar has been, usually on the lower part of the shoulders, then sore shoulders should be suspected. The relevant areas are likely to feel warm to the back of the hand. If left unattended these damp patches may still be there in the morning and in that case this definitely means sore shoulders. A cooling, skin hardening lotion should be applied and under no circumstances should the animal be driven for about a week. The skin will eventually harden and small crinkles under the coat may be noticed. Eventually, little flakes of scurf will appear on the surface of the coat. As soon as any evidence of sore shoulders has been seen, the cause must be put right and recurrence should be prevented. Changing from a full collar to a breast collar or vice versa can help by putting pressure onto different areas, as can padding a breast collar with sheepskin. The animal must be taken out with lighter loads and for shorter distances, over easier terrain, until the shoulders have hardened properly. In order to try to prevent sore shoulders, the lining of the collar must be kept scrupulously clean and soft. It is also essential, if the horse is soft and unfit, to apply a little skin hardening lotion obtainable from your veterinary surgeon, before the horse is first driven. It must, of course, be given time to dry before the animal is harnessed.

Putting on the saddle, crupper and full breeching

The saddle, crupper and breeching (if full breeching is used) are put on in one unit. Various methods, all of which are acceptable, are employed. Some people prefer to buckle the girth loosely when the saddle is put on, in order to prevent it from slipping off the horse's back whilst the crupper and breeching are being put into place. Others prefer to leave the saddle ungirthed, enabling the crupper to be put on without undoing the back strap buckle. The method used depends largely on the experience of the handler and the animal. If the horse is young, or likely to jump about, then it is safer to secure the saddle before putting on the crupper. If the crupper dock is stitched to the crupper back strap, it is necessary to loosen the crupper back strap in order to get the crupper under the tail. If the crupper dock is fastened to the crupper back strap by one or two buckles then the nearside

13 Left: *Putting on a crupper by using the buckle.*

14 Below: *Putting on the crupper, which is stitched to the back strap, by folding the tail.*

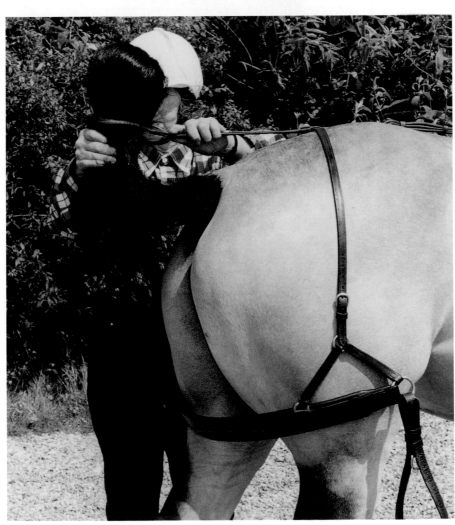

45

buckle is undone and the crupper dock is passed easily under the dock. Whichever method is used, it is essential to take great care when putting the crupper onto the horse. *Never* stand directly behind the horse; a kick, in this vulnerable position, could prove fatal. Always stand to one side where a kick is less likely to be harmful.

If the weather is cold, or the horse is sensitive, it is a good plan to warm the crupper in the hand before passing it under the dock. Cold leather against a warm dock can cause resentment. The alternative is to sew an offcut of sheepskin around the crupper dock, for everyday driving at home, during the winter. It is essential to make sure that the crupper dock is correctly positioned right under the top of the tail. Novices tend to neglect this and the animal suffers considerable discomfort if the crupper dock is not high enough. It is also important to see that all the tail hairs are eased out from the crupper. Failure to do this can result in sores developing and may cause kicking. If the crupper dock is sewn to the back strap, the tail has to be folded, in order to get it through the crupper dock. The easiest method is to take the tail, just below the dock, and twist the hair round to make a kind of rope. Then this is folded in half like darning wool going through a needle. The tail is lifted up firmly and threaded through the crupper dock which is brought upwards until it sits in place and the hairs of the tail are pulled right through. It is then necessary to hold the back strap, while the hairs at the top of the tail are tidied, otherwise the crupper is apt to slide back down the tail. Still holding the back strap, the saddle is lifted up and put down in place on the horse's back. It must not be dragged forward as this will rough up the hairs and may result in a sore back.

The saddle must fit the horse properly. If it is made on a traditional tree then the width of this tree should relate to the width of the animal's back. A wide animal should have a saddle with a wide tree. If a narrow-treed saddle is used, it could pinch. If a wide saddle is put onto a horse with a narrow back, then the saddle will bear down and almost certainly bruise the spine. This could lead to a raw area and the horse will end up with tell-tale white marks around the backbone. There is often a tendency for the saddle to be placed too far forward. This could put pressure onto the spine of a high-withered animal and the belly band will chafe the area around the elbows when going down hills, and cause soreness. Also, if the saddle is put on too far forward, the animal

15 *A correctly fitting saddle.*

will appear to be long in the back, even if he is not. The saddle should be placed in the area where a stable roller would be put, when using a rug.

If a false martingale is worn, the girth is put through the martingale loop before it is buckled to the girth point. Care must be taken not to pinch the horse when buckling the girth to the girth point. It is best to keep one hand behind the straps whilst the other hand does the buckling and this will ensure that the animal is not pinched. The tightness can be compared with the girth of a riding saddle before mounting. It is not necessary to girth too tightly. It should be just tight enough to keep the saddle securely in position. The tightness of the back strap should be enough to ensure that the crupper and saddle are held in place. A rough guide is the hand held sideways between the horse's loins and the back strap.

The belly band is passed through the loop on the outer side of the centre of the girth. Cheap harness is often made without this loop and

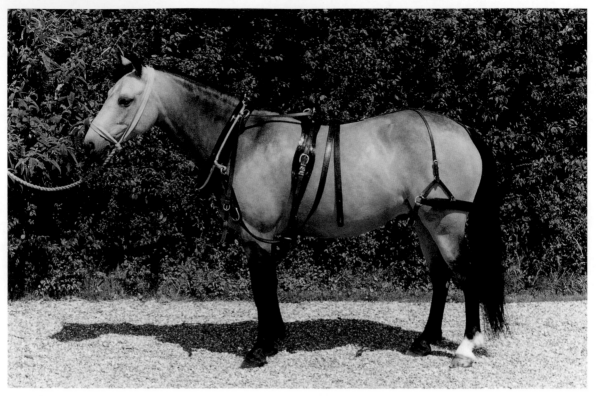

16 *The collar, saddle, reins, crupper and breeching in place with the belly band buckled loosely.*

in this case the belly band can then work its way backwards. The result can look a little like a cinch seen on a rodeo horse. If a false martingale is being used, the belly band is passed through the loop on the martingale. The belly band is buckled loosely to the point of the back band which makes it easier when the time comes to put the shafts through the tugs. If the belly band is buckled tightly, it is very difficult to get the shaft points into the tugs and if it is left undone, it tends to bang on the horse's front legs when he is led to the vehicle. Also, when putting to, if the belly band is undone, it is possible for the cart to be tipped right over backwards should the horse misbehave.

If Tilbury tugs are used it is easier to make one tug into a loop so that the shaft on that side can be put through the tug. The belly band can already be buckled to that side and the other tug can be left open in readiness for putting to.

Whilst the saddle and crupper are being put in place, the breeching seat lies over the quarters. The position should be about half way

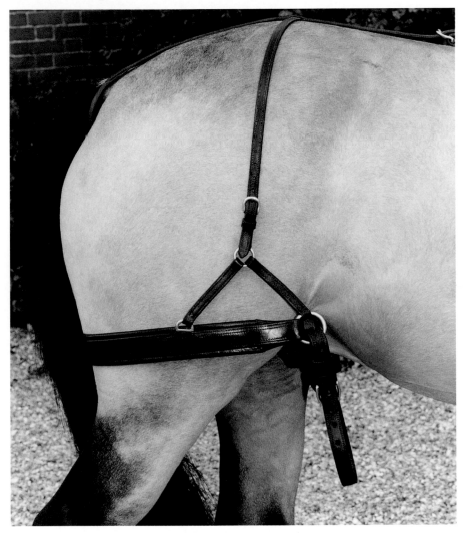

17 *The breeching in the correct position.*

between the widest and narrowest part of the hindquarters. If the seat is too high, there is the danger of it riding upwards and getting caught under the tail which could lead to kicking. If it is too low, it could push the horse's hind legs right under him in descending a steep hill. The seat should lie in a position in which the animal is able to put his weight against it to hold his load either in stopping or down a hill. This is why breeching seats are generally made with plenty of padding. There can be a lot of weight to be taken by the hindquarters, if the load is heavy and the hill is steep.

Putting on the reins

The reins are put on next. If the bridle is put on before the reins, there is the danger of it becoming broken or damaged in the short time that the handler turns round to get the reins. One strategic rub of a blinker stay where it is stitched into the blinker will almost certainly result in damage as the stitching or the leather will be torn. It is possible for a rosette to have its dee broken off the back with a quick rub of an itchy head against a solid object.

The reins can be laid over the horse's back in preparation for putting them on. It is often simplest to have them unbuckled at the hand end, as this saves having to worry about twists. They can be buckled later. It is usual to put the rein which has the little buckle at the hand end on the offside. Although this is not a matter of great importance when harnessing a single, it will be important when the time comes to harness a pair. Some reins are made without a central buckle. This is a nuisance as twists often occur and have to be taken out at the bridle end of the reins. Very often, though, such reins are of poor quality and so unpleasant to handle that they need to be replaced. Some reins are made of webbing and are not as comfortable to handle as those which are made of leather. The choice of reins depends entirely on individual needs. A young person with small hands will probably favour leather reins made to the width of three-quarters of an inch. The author has all her reins made of seven-eighths of an inch width leather. Men very often prefer reins which are an inch wide. Some reins are of plaited leather, others have a strip of leather sewn down the centre of the leather rein. Some are of very soft folded leather from the centre splice to the hand. A good pair of leather reins will last for a lifetime, apart from the renewal of the billets when they become worn, so it is well worth spending the money on this piece of harness which plays such a large part in the comfort of driving. Each rein is passed from the rear, to the front, going through the saddle terrets and collar terrets before being left with enough hanging down to reach the bridle. The ends can then be folded and put through the saddle terret ready for mounting. Whether this is to be on the nearside terret or the offside terret will depend on from which side the Whip is planning to mount.

As a young child in London, the author always mounted from the nearside because, when delivering milk, this was the obvious thing to do; she was likely to get knocked down by a car if she had mounted from

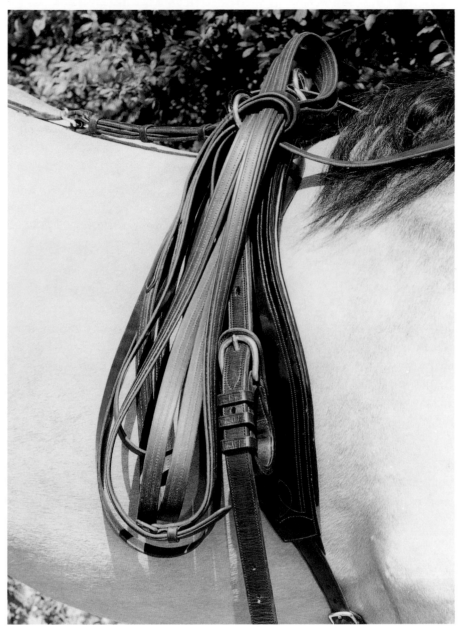

18 *The reins folded through the offside terret.*

the traffic side. However, when she came to be taught to drive by Bert Barley, the carriage was always mounted from the offside, as in coaching, when the coachman mounted on the same side as his box seat. Sandy Watney always mounted his carriages from the offside, whether the Red Rover Coach or an exercise vehicle. Quite understandably, horse breakers frequently mount from the nearside as it is from that side that they are walking alongside the horse prior to mounting.

There are various ways of folding reins into the terret, or the back strap of the crupper, in order to keep them off the ground and from getting trodden on. One method, which the author uses, is to fold the reins, with the nearside rein on top of the offside rein, just beyond the central splice. A bend is made and this loop is passed through the terret. Another loop is made about a foot from the end of the reins and this is put through the first loop. The reins are then pulled a little to tighten them and they are held securely in place. When the time comes to mount, the hand end is pulled and all is released with the nearside rein on top of the offside rein ready to be taken in the hand in preparation for driving. Some drivers like to buckle the ends of their reins together and others prefer not to do this. Some fear that if the reins are buckled and the vehicle should turn over, they could get a foot in the reins and be dragged. Other people say that if the reins are unbuckled, there is a grave danger of dropping one which could prove disastrous. The compromise is to put the point, at the end of the rein, through the keeper by the buckle. This holds the end in place but it would slip out in the case of an emergency.

Putting on the bridle

The bridle is put on last. Some people prefer to put the bridle on as soon as possible, in order to control the animal if circumstances are causing problems. This is understandable but the difficulties are that, unlike a riding bridle, there are no reins attached so something like a head collar rope has to be used. Also, of course there is no question of putting a full collar on over a driving bridle. Great care has to be taken, once the bridle is on, that it does not get broken. The horse cannot be tied up. He has to be held by someone other than the person who is putting on the rest of the harness. It is for these reasons that it is usual to leave the bridle until last when harnessing, and to take it off first when unharnessing.

The bridle is put on in the same way as a riding bridle. Care must be taken in putting the bit into the animal's mouth. Beginners tend to be unintentionally careless in the way in which they bridle their horse. The animal soon objects to this rough treatment and becomes difficult to bridle. It is essential that the horse's mouth is opened to enable the bit to be slipped in, without banging the teeth. If there is any sound of the bit against the teeth, then pain is being caused. The simplest way is to stand on the nearside and take the top of the head piece in the right hand. The bridle is then hung in front of and a little below the horse's face. Various fingers can be used to open the horse's mouth. One way is for the thumb of the left hand to lie under the mouth piece of the bit in order to guide it towards the mouth at the same time as the middle finger of the same hand slips into the offside corner of the mouth, against the bars (where there are no teeth with the average mare and only the tushes with a male horse). Usually, once the horse feels the finger on the corner he will open his mouth and the bridle can be pulled up by the right hand and the bit will slip into the open mouth. Animals who are carefully treated in this way are unlikely to be a problem to bridle. It is just as important, when the bridle is taken off, that care should be taken not to rush the operation and drag the bit out of the horse's mouth before he has had time to open it. It is for this reason that the bridle should always be put on and taken off with the noseband unbuckled and a curb chain unfastened. A tight noseband prevents the animal from opening his mouth and a fastened curb chain gets caught in the chin groove. Once the bridle is on the horse's head, a check has to be made to ensure that it is fitting correctly.

The brow band should be of the right length so that it is not pulling the rosettes and head piece forwards onto the base of the ears which would cause discomfort. If it is very much too large, it will allow the head piece to slip back and the cheeks of the bridle to gape. This could permit the horse to see behind his blinkers and cause an accident. It is essential that the blinkers are fitted correctly. With good quality harness, the blinkers are based on metal or glass fibre plates. These keep the leather in a concave shape and this is comfortable for the horse. Unfortunately, a lot of cheap harness is being made with flat blinkers which, in some cases, touch the eye lashes and even parts of the eyes. The centre of the horse's eye should coincide with the centre of the blinker. He should not be able to see above, or below, and there should be no contact with the eyes on the inside of the blinkers. A lot of animals have to put up with great discomfort owing to ill-fitting bridles that come with poor quality harness. The height of the blinkers is adjusted by the top buckles on the cheek pieces. The wearing of

19 *A correctly fitting bridle with the reins buckled to the rough cheek position on a Liverpool bit.*

20 *The bridle from the front to show the correct position of the blinkers.*

blinkers originates from team-driving traditions. If all four of a team were in open bridles and one was being lazy whilst the other three were going freely on, it would be almost impossible to use the whip on the lazy horse. As the thong of the whip was being unfolded, the three onward going horses would go even faster and the idle horse would probably carry on being lazy. It would be difficult to hit him without upsetting the other three even more. If, on the other hand, all four were in blinkers, the whip could be quietly unfolded and the idle horse hit without the other three taking too much notice. The lazy horse could then be made to do his share of the work. The tradition of blinkers has stayed and although some horses prefer to work in open bridles, it is generally accepted that blinkers be worn. Horses who are not accustomed to working without blinkers can become unbelievably afraid if they see the wheels of their vehicle rotating behind them. The top part of the wheel travels forward towards the horse giving the appearance that it is chasing or even overhauling him. Flight is the horse's instant reaction. For this reason, it is important that the blinkered bridle is *never* removed from the horse, whilst he is still put to the vehicle. Numerous bad accidents are caused, every year, by people who break this golden rule. Some people use open cup blinkers, similar to those used for racing, to enable animals to see more when it comes to the cross-country phase of an event, whilst still restricting the rear vision. However, horses, such as those used by the army, often work in open bridles. These are usually in gun carriages and ridden and driven by postillions, so different methods apply.

The noseband must fit correctly. It is essential that the keepers, or slots, at the sides are in the correct place to allow the cheeks to lie in a straight line down towards the bit. If the front of the noseband is too short, the cheeks will be pulled forward and the bit may be tilted. This, in turn, brings the blinkers forward onto the eyes. Also, a noseband which is too short can have an adverse effect on the action of the bit. The rear of the noseband should fit snugly against the jaw and neither be too loose nor too tight. The height of the bit is altered by the cheek piece buckles above the noseband. The type of bit which is used will depend on whichever suits the horse the best.

The throatlash is fastened, just tightly enough to hold the bridle in place. If it is too tight, it will press into the throat and the horse will not be able to carry his head or flex his jaw comfortably. There is nowadays a tendency to keep the head collar on, under the bridle, for work at home. This can cause discomfort as buckles dig in sometimes and prevent the bridle from sitting neatly in place.

The use of a wide neck strap can be preferable to a head collar for such occasions as with young horses or driving through hazards at an event. This can lie round the throat without digging in or hurting and the throatlash can be threaded through, which will keep the bridle in place when it might otherwise have been rubbed or pulled off. Of course this cannot be used for showing in private driving classes. Once the bridle is on, and the curb chain is hooked and checked for comfort, then the reins can be buckled to the bit. The horse is now ready to be put to.

Bitting

The Liverpool bit is used more than any other with single private driving turn-outs. Its versatility enables it to be employed for most horses. The action can be similar to that of a snaffle or pelham, depending on where the reins are buckled to the bit. There is a 'key' to

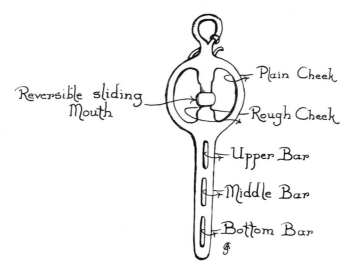

Fig. 11 *Cheek of Liverpool bit with rein positions named*

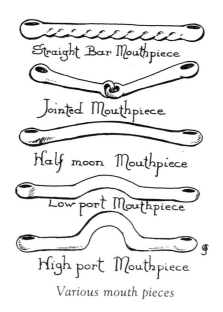

Various mouth pieces

every horse's mouth and this must be found. Mouth pieces of Liverpool bits are made from rubber and nylon, as well as from stainless steel and nickel. Stainless steel bits are generally safer than solid nickel which has been known to break. Liverpool bits can be obtained with straight bar mouth pieces as well as jointed, half moon, low port and high port. The lengths of the cheeks, both above and below the mouth piece, vary to give differing degrees of leverage. The variety of Liverpool bits is so great that there is one to suit almost every kind of mouth.

The severity of the bit depends mainly on the mouth piece and the position in which the reins are buckled. Of course, the adjustment of the curb, and whether it is of chain, leather or elastic, also plays a considerable part in the degree of severity. Some Liverpool bits have a choice of five positions for the buckling of the reins, from the mildest when the reins are buckled onto the rings, known as plain cheek, through rough cheek to upper, middle and lower or bottom bar for the greatest leverage and degree of severity.

The mildest Liverpool bit would be one which has a rubber or nylon mouth piece, used with an elastic curb and the reins buckled to plain cheek. Pressure is taken mainly on the tongue. The curb is non-operative. The action can be compared with that of a rubber or nylon snaffle. A bit with a jointed mouth piece, gives a nutcracker type of action on the tongue and pressure is also put onto the corners of the horse's mouth. This can be useful in helping to raise the head. Some horses favour a half moon, or mullen, mouth piece, but are too strong for rubber or nylon, so a metal bit of this shape may be suitable. Many horses go best in a mouth piece with a low port. The tongue lies in the arch of the port and a lot of the pressure of the bit is taken on the bars of the mouth. Ported bits are also helpful for use with horses which resist by putting their tongues over the bit as the port makes this disagreeable habit more difficult. A horse with a fleshy tongue generally prefers these to a straight bar which presses on the tongue.

Some straight bar bits can be reversed to give a rough side designed to be used for horses which pull hard. It is usually better, though, to tighten the noseband than to increase the severity of the pressure on the mouth. Most pulling tends to be caused by animals who open their mouths, cross their jaws and set their heads and necks against their driver's hands. It is better to deal with this problem, in preventing the mouth from opening so wide, than to inflict pain which will just deaden and callous the tongue, bars and chin groove to result in an even harder mouth.

The curb should come into action, in the chin groove, when the cheeks of the bit are at forty-five degrees to the mouth. It is essential, when hooking the curb onto the bit, to see that the chain, leather or elastic is lying flat and is neither too tight or too loose. Too tight a curb will deaden the chin groove and cease to have any effect. It can even develop a corn over a long period. Too loose a curb chain will be non-operative. When the reins are buckled onto the cheeks, the top eye of the bit will be seen to tilt forward as the curb is brought into action. This puts pressure onto the cheeks of the bridle which, in turn, presses onto the horse's poll to help to lower the head.

Wilson snaffles were, and still are, frequently used with trade turn-outs. They are made with both jointed and straight bar mouth pieces. There are two floating rings on the mouth piece which also has a ring at each end. The cheek pieces of the bridle are buckled to the loose, floating, rings and the reins are normally buckled to both rings. However, if severe action is required, using a jointed mouth piece the reins can be buckled to the rings at each end of the mouth piece and not to the floating rings. This puts pressure onto the sides of the mouth as well as putting a nutcracker action on the tongue, when contact is increased on the reins. The type of bit which is used will very often depend on the conformation of the horse and time must be spent finding that which is most comfortable for the animal concerned.

Fig. 12 *Wilson snaffle*

Leading out of the stable

21 *Leading the pony from the stable.*

Great care has to be taken when leading the harnessed horse out of the stable. It must be remembered that he can no longer see backwards owing to his blinkers. The best method is to stand in front of him and line him up with the centre of the doorway. He can then be brought carefully forward and any chance of the tug, or his hip or the loin strap touching the door post will be avoided as the handler takes a few steps backwards, keeping the horse straight as he comes through the doorway. If the doorway is narrow, or the animal is nervous or young, it is safer to put the bridle on outside. Once an animal has had a fright from being taken through a door carelessly it is quite likely that he will rush for the rest of his life. This can result in such injuries as a dropped hip. It will almost certainly lead to broken harness. If a tug gets caught, this will pull the back band and that, in turn, can tear the top of the saddle.

Choosing a vehicle

The type of vehicle purchased will depend upon which aspect of the sport is being pursued. In any case, it is usually necessary to have an everyday exercise vehicle. It will often be found that all good intentions of having and housing only one carriage will disappear as involvement in the sport increases. The family's cars tend to end up in the driveway as all garage space becomes filled with precious carriages.

If showing is to be the main interest, then a suitable vehicle such as a Gig, Dog Cart or Phaeton will be needed. Such a carriage cannot be used for exercising as it will get scratched, or for the marathon section of a driving trial, when a specialised vehicle is needed to withstand the rigours of such a competition. If this 'marathon' vehicle is to be used for 'presentation and dressage' phases of an event, it will inevitably need to be thoroughly cleaned and touched-up before a competition. The horse has to be kept fit during this time so an exercise carriage is necessary. Already we can see that two carriages are essential for anyone who plans to compete.

It is probably wisest for the newcomer to start with an exercise vehicle or with a modern cross-country vehicle. Numerous carriage builders, whose names and addresses can be obtained from the secretaries of driving societies throughout the world, are employing modern materials and techniques to produce suitable vehicles for use in horse-driving trials. Metal wheels with disc brakes and roller bearings are quite usual, as are bodies made with metal panels. Vehicles are often built to specific widths and weights to comply with driving trials rules. Many of the builders are also competitors, so have first-hand knowledge of the requirements of their customers.

Exercise vehicles are being built to a large number of patterns. Some have pneumatic tyres, the main disadvantage of which is that they can puncture; a noisy blow out can be disastrous with a young horse. Pneumatic-tyred wheels are almost always of less diameter than traditional wheels which has the effect, for a cart which is balanced on the level, of being shaft heavy when going down hill and tending to tip up when going up hill. Some exercise carts are badly built, so care has to be taken before purchasing. It is very important, in the case of a two-wheeler, to see that the balance is correct, for one which is shaft

22 *The author's Spider Phaeton which was made to measure for her and her ponies by Mark Broadbent of Fenix Carriages.*

heavy will always be unsatisfactory. It will probably give the horse a sore back and will also shake the driver and passenger. Some have very little springing and jar the occupants considerably. A few are built with no side or back rails to the seat. This is extremely dangerous as it is quite easy for the driver and passenger to be either tipped off the side or thrown off the back.

One certain way of purchasing a vehicle which will fit all the desired requirements is to have it made to measure by a specialised and well-established carriage builder. The buyer will probably be able to choose exactly the type of carriage which is wanted and the craftsman will be likely to draw plans to enable the vehicle to be made to satisfy every wish. Some carriage builders will even go to the lengths of making a lifesize replica in hard board so that the exact shape and proportions can be agreed. In some ways, it is like having a suit of clothes made, in that the purchaser will be required to go for fittings to ensure that, stage by stage, the vehicle will fit him and his horse. In the case of a two-wheeler, the correct balance will be ensured. Choice of colour for paint and trimming will be entirely that of the buyer. Such a carriage will, of course, be expensive, but the vehicle will last for well over a lifetime if it is cared for and housed properly.

It is best when purchasing a showing vehicle to choose one which is suitable for the type of animal concerned. Gigs are favoured by a number of people. They come in many kinds of shapes and sizes. All have two wheels and most have two forward facing seats which cannot be altered for balance. It is therefore very important that the carriage has been correctly built and does not ride shaft heavy or light. It must, of course, fit the horse. It is also essential for the driver to try it for size. A lot of gigs tend to be short of leg room.

Some gigs, like the Dennett Gig, are named after their type of spring-ing, others, like the Spider Gig and Skeleton Gig, from their light looking outline. The Stanhope Gig takes its name from Lord Stanhope, for whom it was designed, and the Tilbury Gig from the carriage builder of that name. The Round Backed Gig and Bucket Seat Gig are named from their body shape, as is the Well Bottom Gig. All of these are suitable for showing in private driving or Concours d'Elegance classes. Some judges favour four-wheelers in a Concours d'Elegance class. A vehicle such as a Spider Phaeton with a quality single or pair can make a very elegant picture. Country Carts such as Dog Carts and Norfolk Carts are suitable for private driving classes. Varnished editions of these can look extremely smart especially when used with a suitable country type of animal wearing highly polished brown harness.

Governess Carts are useful for taking small children for drives but they are not particularly favoured in the show ring. They are very suitable for use with children because young people can mount from the rear door away from the dangers of the pony's hind legs. The children can be shut into the cart and taken for a drive without the worry that they might fall out. Governess Carts are not suitable for use with young or difficult horses because of the driving position; the Whip has to sit slightly sideways and it is not easy to get enough purchase with the feet should the horse start to pull. Also, there is the added problem of trying to open the rear door, whilst holding onto a pulling horse. For all these reasons it may be unwise to pay too much money for a Governess

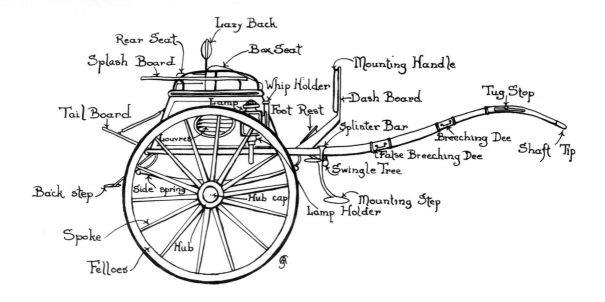

Labels on figure:
Rear Seat, Lazy Back, Box Seat, Splash Board, Mounting Handle, Whip Holder, Dash Board, Tug Stop, Lamp, Foot Rest, Splinter Bar, Tail Board, Louvres, Breeching Dee, Shaft Tip, False Breeching Dee, Swingle Tree, Back step, Side spring, Hub cap, Mounting Step, Lamp Holder, Spoke, Hub, Felloes

Fig. 13 *Parts of a two-wheeled Dog Cart*

Cart. Some beginners make the mistake of buying such a vehicle and then spending far more than it is worth in having it beautifully restored by a specialist craftsman. This is only to be recommended if the intention is to keep the vehicle for years of pleasure but is not sensible if the hope is to make a large profit.

If a vehicle is to be bought second-hand, it is important to ensure that it will fit the animal as well as the driver. The ideal answer is to put the three together to try for size and, in the case of a two-wheeler, for balance. This may be possible if buying as a result of an advertisement, when the vendor may allow the purchaser to take his animal for a trial drive; however, it is not possible when purchasing at an auction.

It is a good idea, before going to see a vehicle, to put the saddle onto the horse with the tugs lying in the correct position, and to take the measurement from the bottom of the tug to the ground. If a vehicle which fits is already owned, this is relatively simple; it is wise to take all the measurements of the shafts. It is useful to note the length from the shaft tip to the splinter bar together with the width at the shaft tip, tug stops, breeching dees and splinter bar. On arrival at the sale, suitable vehicles can be seen and measured. When taking the height measurement, be sure to hold the shafts in the position, in the case of a

64

two-wheeler, which makes the seat absolutely level, before comparing the height from the tug stop to the ground with the measurement which was taken with the horse in its saddle at home. The lengths and widths of the shafts on traditional vehicles are usually fairly standard if the carriage has been built by a specialised craftsman. However, there are a lot of vehicles which have had their shafts altered to fit long, short, fat and thin animals. Also, a number of competitors now have competition carriages made with very short shafts for the marathon phase and animals are being squeezed up against dashboards in some cases. So, it is as well to have plenty of measurements before setting off to buy a second-hand carriage.

If the vehicle is a four-wheeler, of course the seat remains level on the body at all times. The shafts are fixed to the front of the vehicle and can be raised and lowered as required. The measurements of the shafts, in general, may act as a guide. A problem which can occur when buying at a sale, is that it is possible that shafts not originally intended for the particular vehicle being sold may be put with it for sale purposes. The general size of the vehicle in proportion to the animal concerned is critical for showing. These proportions are becoming less important for competing in horse-driving trials when it is the specific widths and weights which cause concern.

One helpful measurement, when purchasing a traditional four-wheeler, is the height of the fixing for the traces. If these are too high, then the line from the collar through the traces will go upwards towards the front of the carriage and the draught will be adversely affected. Such a carriage is likely to be too big for the animal concerned. However, a lot of modern four-wheelers, made for cross-country events, are now fitted with low swingle trees to slope the draught down from the shoulder to give a low line to make pulling easier for the horse on the marathon.

If the vehicle is of a traditional type, one can look to see if there are any wooden blocks between the axle and the spring to heighten the body. Bear in mind that these could be removed. If these are taken out, the carriage will automatically be lowered. Equally, if there is only about half an inch of wood between the axle and the spring, then an inch or so could be added to bring it up that much. Beware of vehicles which have too much blocking up as this can be a very weak area and could cause an accident. Be careful, too, of a newly but badly painted

23 *The block which is sometimes found between the axle and the spring.*

vehicle. The paint could be covering a mass of putty or similar filler which will probably drop out as soon as the vehicle is used and could cause a horrible accident. Hubs, the bottoms of spokes where they join the felloes, and areas in the felloes near the metal channels, or tyres, are common places for filler to be put by unscrupulous people. It is far safer, in the case of a second-hand traditional carriage, to purchase one which is in need of paint so that the condition of the wood can be clearly seen. Obviously, if the vehicle is painted to a high standard, it is likely to be sound. No true craftsman would be prepared to spend hundreds of hours painting, and rubbing down, on an unsound surface. As with purchasing a horse, when it comes to buying a carriage it can very much be a case of 'buyer beware'.

Care of a vehicle

Someone once said that as much care should be taken of a carriage as a gentleman would take of his wardrobe. A carriage should, ideally, be housed in a building which is free from damp, heat, ammonia fumes, vermin and direct sunlight. If the atmosphere is too warm, as in some centrally heated museums, the wood can shrink and cracks will appear. Dampness causes metal parts to rust and the sun's rays will quickly fade the paint. Rats, mice and moths delight in cushions and so all removable upholstery should be stored in trunks with camphor balls. A watch needs to be kept for signs of woodworm.

If the vehicle is a two-wheeler with wooden shafts, it should not be left with the shafts on the ground since a bend could develop at the splinter bar. Shafts can also be trodden on, or run over, damaged or broken. When not in use the carriage should be tipped backwards with the shafts in the air. A piece of cloth-covered wood, approximately ten centimetres (four inches) by five centimetres (two inches) in thickness and about one hundred and twenty-two centimetres (four feet) long, should be placed over the axle. The back of the body, or the rear spring, then rests on the wood and the weight of the vehicle is taken on the wood as the end rests on the ground. It is essential to put triangular-shaped chocks under the wheels before the vehicle is tipped back; failure to do this can result in the vehicle running forward and tipping right over until it rests on its back, with the shafts in the air. Once this has happened, the average woman will be unable to get it down again on her own. The vehicle and shafts should be covered with light cloths to keep off the dust. Felt is best avoided since it will attract moths, whose grubs can damage leather and varnish. If the vehicle has rubber shod wheels it should be moved from time to time to prevent flat surfaces from developing on the solid rubber tyres where the wheel is on the ground.

When the carriage is cleaned, it is essential to use plenty of water to remove grit, sand or mud, to prevent them from scratching the paint. A special cloth should be kept for any areas where there may be traces of oil, such as at the ends of the springs. Once the vehicle is thoroughly clean, it can be dried with a chamois leather and polished with a soft cloth. Patent-leather areas such as the splash and dashboards can be cleaned with patent shoe cleaner or just a soft cloth. Metal polish must be used sparingly on shaft fittings and rein rails; to use too much can cause layers of white to develop on the wood, paint or leather. Cushions must be brushed. The seat straps must be kept well fed with saddle soap, as should any other non-patent-leather parts such as cee springs or hoods. Hoods are best left up when the vehicle is stored as this will help to prevent cracking. A little oil can be put on the ends of the springs, around the shackles. The hub caps, in traditional vehicles, can be topped up with thick oil; to do this, take an octagonal wheel wrench, which matches the cap for size, and rotate in an anti-clockwise direction to remove the cap, pour oil into the recess in the cap, and replace it. As the wheel rotates, the oil will work its way along the ridge in the axle and keep it lubricated.

It is a good idea to check, from time to time, that the wheels are running freely. First, put the shafts onto a trestle or shaft rest of some kind and place chocks against the wheel – in the case of a two-wheeler – or wheels – in the case of a four-wheeler – which are not being checked. Then, put a wheel jack under the axle and jack up the vehicle so that the wheel is off the ground. The wheel can then be spun and if it feels stiff to turn, further investigation is necessary. To take the wheel off, the vehicle should be let down onto the ground again, the hub cap removed with the wheel wrench and the vehicle jacked up again. If the wheel is on a Collinge axle, a split pin will be seen at the end of the axle. It is put there to prevent the nuts, which are retaining the wheel, from coming off. This pin must be removed, using a pair of pliers. There is a hexagon-shaped nut which will probably have a left-handed thread. This must now be taken off. Next, there will be a hexagon-shaped nut which is a little larger and of the opposite thread from the one which has just been removed; this must be taken off. The purpose of these opposite threaded nuts is to prevent vibration from loosening them both. Care must be taken not to damage the sides or threads of these nuts as they may be expensive to replace. The wheel can now slide off the axle but some difficulty may be experienced as there is a collet still in place, on the axle. The collet is a metal collar with a flat on one side to match a flat on the axle at that point, the purpose of which is to prevent the nut from being influenced by the wheel's rotation. Once the wheel is off, a leather washer will be exposed, which regulates the end play of the wheel and prevents surplus oil from running out over

24 *A wheel jack in position.*

the inside of the wheel. If this washer is worn, some play will develop and the wheel, when it is on the ground, will have some sideways movement. In the show ring, some judges have a tendency to come up to competitors and to give the carriage wheel a hearty shake. Worn washers cause great delight to these judges, so the answer is to keep the washers renewed as necessary, and avoid this criticism. A shoe repairer or saddler can usually be persuaded to cut replacement washers if the old ones are taken to him as a pattern.

If, when the wheel is taken off the axle, there are signs of rust or black looking grease, the axle must be cleaned with paraffin. The channel along the axle can be filled with thick oil and the wheel put back. Once the nuts are tightened and the split pin returned, be sure to check that the wheel is rotating freely before letting it down off the jack and repeating the process on the other side, or other three wheels in the case of a four-wheeler. Care must be taken when replacing the nuts to adjust them so that the wheel runs freely without excessive end play.

Carriages with Mail axles also have leather washers to take up any surplus end play of the wheel on the axle. The wheels are held on by three bolts which run right through the hub, having nuts at their ends. Once these three nuts are undone, the wheel can be drawn off its axle. Occasionally, there are three nuts on the inner side of the hub, but, unlike the usual Mail axle, there are no bolts going right through the hub. The wheel is removed by undoing those nuts.

Many American carriages have one centre nut which holds the wheel onto the axle. The nuts tighten in the same direction as the wheels rotate, so care must be taken when undoing them to turn the spanner the correct way. These axles can only be lubricated by removing the wheels and greasing, because the nuts are not designed to hold oil as hub caps do.

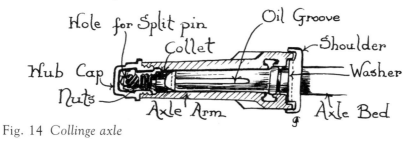

Fig. 14 *Collinge axle*

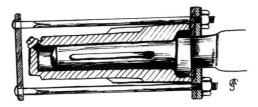

Mail axle

Many of the modern carriages are built with sealed roller bearings on their axles, which were packed with lubricant when they were made. If any attention is needed, it is probably safest to take the vehicle back to the manufacturer who will know exactly how to deal with any problems. Some modern carriages have the outer appearance of having traditional Collinge or Mail axles but are, in fact, built using roller bearings on the axles. So, before embarking on a major operation with spanners, it may be wise to ask the builder which method he has used, under the outward appearance of the traditional hub cap.

If the vehicle is a four-wheeler, it is important to check that the turntable, or fifth wheel as it is also known, is kept well lubricated. This forms a bearing above the front axle for the undercarriage assembly, and if it is allowed to become dry, the steering of the vehicle will be adversely affected.

The lamps

25 *An oval-fronted gig lamp.*

A number of carriage builders also make, or supply, lamps to go with their vehicles. It is quite a good idea to purchase the lamps at the same time as the vehicle, as the holders and stems can vary in size. Those which are bought with the carriage will fit the holders which have been put onto the vehicle.

It is correct to carry lamps on smart occasions when the turn-out is being shown in Private driving or Concours d'Elegance classes. Whether they are of square, oval or round design will usually depend on the lines of the carriage with which they are used as will the size chosen. The main thing is that they should be neat and unfussy. The polished metal parts need to match those of the rest of the vehicle and the harness, whether of brass or of white metal such as silver-plate or nickel. Large ornate lamps are not suitable for light private driving vehicles. These are employed with carriages used for ceremonial and similar occasions.

It is not sensible to venture out at night on public roads with two-candle-power lighting on the carriage. It is however quite surprising, on a dark night, how much light is thrown both forwards and sideways by one candle being reflected from the silver inside a carriage lamp. While this may be adequate, from the Whip's point of view, in that he can see well enough to travel at a steady six to nine miles an hour, it is not safe on a public highway. A car driver approaching from behind at perhaps sixty miles an hour is unlikely to see the small red light which is shining from the rear of a one-candle-power lamp.

It is safest never to drive at night with a horse and carriage on a public road. If an occasion arises when it is essential to drive on a road in poor daylight visibility it is best to have red reflectors fixed to the rear of the carriage. In fact, many carriage builders are now fitting these as a standard accessory. It is wise to wear reflective clothing at all times when driving on public roads. Various reflecting bands suitable for use with horse-drawn carriages can be obtained from motor accessory shops.

Putting to

26 *Putting to.*

When the horse is put to a light two-wheeled vehicle it is preferable to bring the carriage up to the horse rather than to teach the horse to step back towards the vehicle. Once the horse gets into the habit of stepping back at this time he is likely accidentally to step on and damage a shaft tip. The horse can be held by an assistant whilst the driver brings the vehicle up from behind, taking care to keep the shafts up so that they do not dig into the horse's hindquarters in the process. The shafts are put through the tugs. This will be found to be much easier if the belly band has been buckled loosely because if it is tight, the manoeuvrability of the tugs is greatly restricted and difficulty will be experienced in putting the shaft tips through the tugs. The vehicle is drawn forward until the tugs rest against the tug stops on both sides.

The traces are always hooked on next and care must be taken to see that they are not twisted. Each one is passed inside the belly band if open tugs are being used. The only time that traces run outside the belly band is with Tilbury tugs, which are used mostly with four-wheeled vehicles and very rarely with two wheelers. If the vehicle is one of a

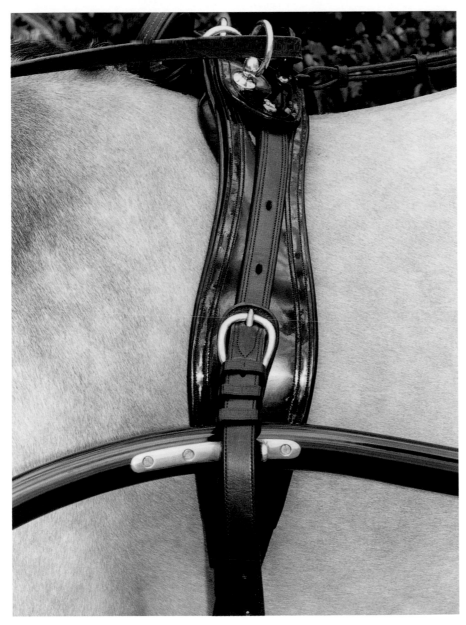

27 *The shaft tug against the tug stop with the back band hanging vertically and the belly band buckled loosely.*

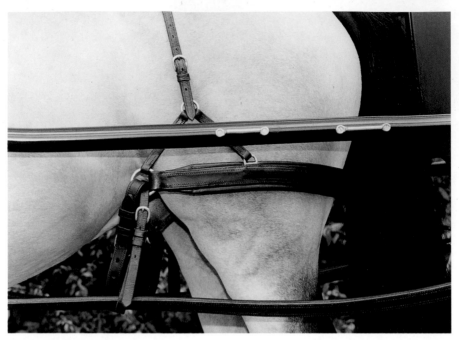

28 *The trace is passed through the trace carrier before being hooked onto the swingle tree. The breeching strap is not buckled yet.*

29 *The trace is hooked onto the swingle tree hook.*

modern design which has a low swingle tree, then the traces are passed through loops, known as trace carriers, which hang below the rings on the breeching, before they are fastened to the trace hooks. The purpose of these loops is to keep the traces up when they slacken in going down a hill. There is a danger, if the trace is not held up, of a hind leg getting caught in a loop in the trace. With traditionally designed carriages, the traces lie either through, or above, the breeching straps where these are attached to the shafts. This is not possible if the swingle tree is very low because if the trace is passed through the breeching straps, this prevents the trace from going down in a straight line from the collar to the trace hook. With a two-wheeled vehicle, the traces are always attached first and disconnected last because should the horse step forward when the traces are hooked on, he will take the vehicle with him and the handlers will be able to check the whole turn-out. If, on the other

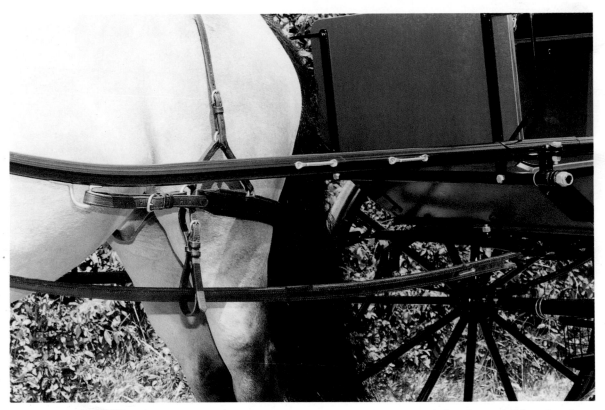

30 *The breeching strap is passed through the under shaft dee with the trace below being held up by the trace carrier. The dees at the rear are for false breeching and the dees between those and the full breeching are for use with a kicking strap.*

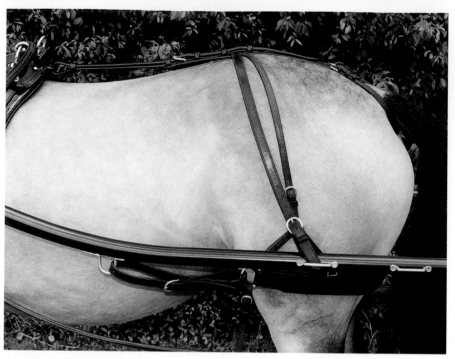

31 *The kicking strap.*

hand, the breeching straps are fastened before the traces, the horse will be half in and half out of the vehicle if he steps forward. The shafts may fall out of the tugs and the horse is just held back by his breeching straps with the shafts on the ground. This will almost certainly result in an accident and a lot of broken equipment. Both traces are slotted onto the trace hooks by the hole at the end, known as the crew hole. If there are two or more crew holes cut in each trace end, the last one should be used. If this should break, then the trace can be let out at the hame tug buckle and the next crew hole can be used. The breeching straps can now be buckled round the shaft, through the breeching dees. Some vehicles have three lots of dees on their shafts. The dees, which are situated about fifty-one centimetres (twenty inches) from the tug stop, with a 14.2 hand animal, are the full breeching dees onto which the breeching straps are buckled. The next pair of dees, situated about thirty centimetres (twelve inches) back from the full breeching dees, are for use with a kicking strap which might be employed for young horses. The rearmost dees, usually placed about thirty-eight centimetres (fifteen inches) forward from the splinter bar, are for false breeching.

Some vehicles have triangular-shaped dees under the shafts, to take the full breeching straps. The purpose of these is to prevent wear on the paint and wood from breeching straps.

There are numerous ways of fixing the breeching straps to the breeching dees on the side of the shafts. The main point to remember is that the strap is passed around the shaft, through the dee, and

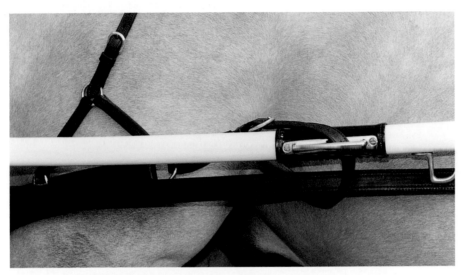

32 *The breeching strap round the shaft and trace, with the breeching strap buckle on top of the shaft.*

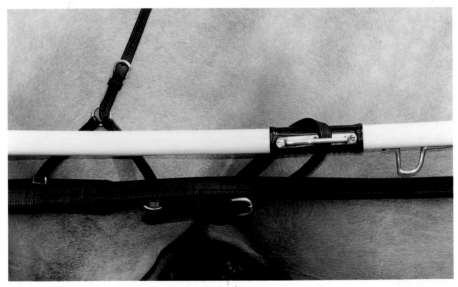

33 *The breeching strap round the shaft and trace with the buckle below the shaft.*

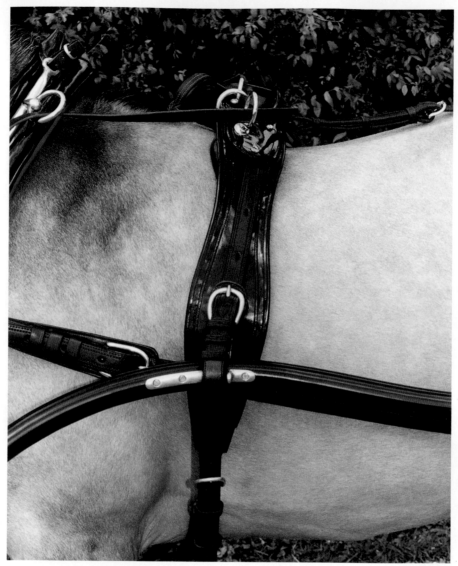

34 *The belly band is tightened a little.*

includes the trace (except with some modern cross-country vehicles), to keep it in position when going down hills. Some people have the breeching strap buckle on top of the shaft. This can cause the paint to become scratched and patent leather on show vehicles to become damaged. Other people prefer to have the buckle below the shaft to prevent this wear. The method used depends on personal choice, and does not matter too much providing that the breeching operates correctly and that the horse is comfortable. Some people run the trace over the top of the breeching straps. This is fine providing that the trace hooks on the vehicle are high. The object of this method is that if the horse should hump his back and try to kick, the traces will tighten, as his head goes down. The traces will bear on the breeching straps, thus putting pressure onto the loin strap. This makes it work like a kicking strap by helping to hold the quarters down.

Once the traces and breeching straps are fastened, the belly band can be tightened a few holes. This must not be too tight, with a two-wheeler, because there has to be some allowance for play as the cart runs along. The tug buckles should chatter with the points gently rising and falling if the vehicle is perfectly balanced, with no weight on either the animal's back or its belly. If the belly band is buckled too tightly, then the vehicle will be held rigidly, making it very uncomfortable for both the driver and the horse. If the belly band is too loose, then the vehicle can float about too much. Should the horse rear and the belly band be very loose, it is possible for the shafts to get caught sideways across the animal's back if he turns as he comes down from his rear.

Taking a single horse out of a two-wheeler is exactly the reverse to putting to after the reins have been folded through the terrets. The belly band is loosened, the breeching straps are undone, the traces are unhooked and the vehicle is pushed back from the horse.

False breeching

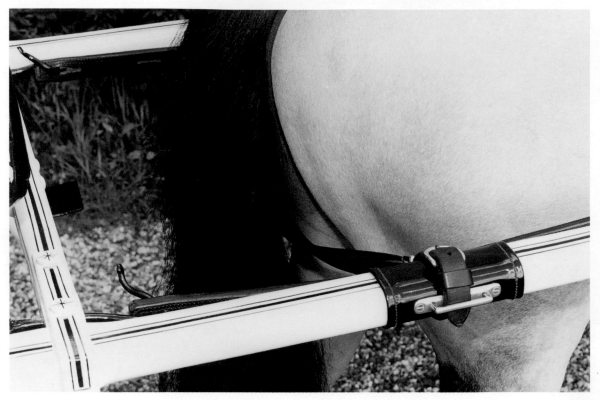

35 *The false breeching in place.*

Some people prefer to use false breeching instead of full breeching. It is safest not to use this kind of breeching with a newly broken animal. The false breeching lies between the shafts, away from the hindquarters. When the animal is checked, or stopped, or when a downhill slope is encountered, the vehicle runs forward causing the false breeching seat to come suddenly into contact with the horse's quarters. Naturally, this can surprise and frighten the animal and could lead to kicking. It is, however, quite acceptable for use with animals who are experienced and unlikely to be alarmed by this sudden contact. The great advantage of a false breeching is that its use cuts down the time which it takes to put to. The breeching remains on the vehicle and is removed periodically for cleaning. The shaft straps of this breeching remain buckled round the shafts, in the rearmost dees. The seat of the breeching is fixed to the straps by two figure-of-eight-shaped metal fittings. This enables the seat to lie flat against the horse's quarters whilst the straps around the shafts can then lie flat. If the kind of two-ringed swivel which is often seen on lungeing reins is used, the seat will then get a half twist which will be very uncomfortable for the horse if he gets the sharp edge against his hindquarters.

When putting to, the traces run through the shaft straps on their way to the trace hooks, on the splinter bar, or swingle tree if it is high enough. If the swingle tree is low, then the traces cannot be passed through the false breeching straps as these would be too high. False breeching can be used for showing but it is not advisable for use if the animal is inclined to be long in the back. Full breeching is preferable for this type of horse because the presence of the loin strap breaks up the apparent length. False breeching is suitable for use with a close-coupled animal, put to a vehicle of traditional type, as it shows the back and quarters to advantage.

Putting to using Tilbury tugs

Putting the horse to a four-wheeled vehicle is a little different from putting to a two-wheeler. The shafts of a traditional four-wheeler are free to go up and down quite independently of the vehicle and so Tilbury tugs are used to hold the shafts steady. When putting to, the horse is led into position, in front of the dashboard, and the shafts are brought down and put into the Tilbury tugs. The shafts are laid into the curves of the tugs so that the tugs rest in front of the tug stops. The points of the leather which are sewn to the outer sides of the tugs are passed over the shafts and through the lower slots in the Tilbury tug buckles. The point straps are then taken down alongside the saddle and passed through loops at the bottom of the saddle skirts before being buckled to the belly band. The belly band is fastened on top of the girth, more tightly than a belly band which is used with open tugs, in order to hold the shafts so as to prevent them from jumping up and down. The traces are fastened next. These lie on the outer sides of the belly band because if they were put on the inside, the dees would probably be torn off the saddle. The breeching straps are buckled in the usual way. In taking off, the breeching is unbuckled first, the traces next

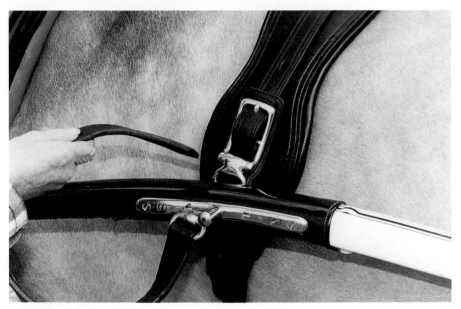

36 *The point strap of the Tilbury tug being put over the shaft.*

84

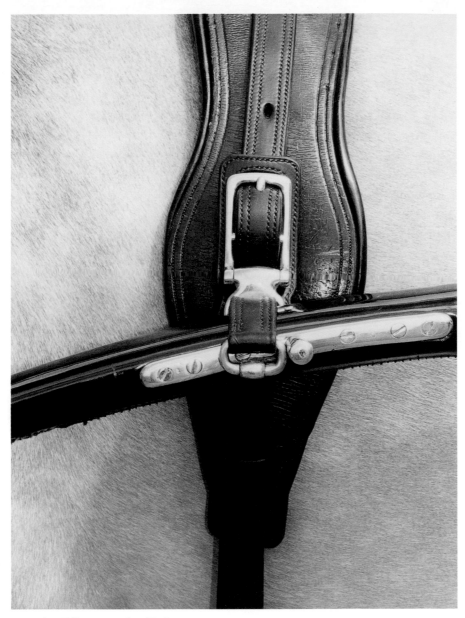

37 *The Tilbury tug buckled in position.*

and the Tilbury tugs are unbuckled from the belly band last. The tug points can then be loosened from the shafts, the shafts lifted upwards and the horse led forward. So, the golden rule of the traces always being fastened to the trace hooks first, with a single turn-out, has an exception. If Tilbury tugs are used, the traces are fastened after the tugs.

Fitting the horse to the harness and the vehicle

Once the horse is put to the vehicle, it is important to check that all is fitting comfortably. Failure to notice that any part of the harness is buckled incorrectly can result in an accident. The best place to start is with the back band. The tugs should lie against the tug stops with the back band perpendicular to the ground when the traces are tight. The simplest way to test this is to push the vehicle backwards until the traces take up the tension and see that the tugs remain in place in front of the tug stops, with the back band at the perpendicular. If the tugs have moved forward along the shafts towards the tips, or the back band hangs behind the perpendicular, then the traces need to be shortened at the tug buckle. A check must be made, at this time, to ensure that the breeching seat is about a hand's width from the hindquarters. If it is any looser, it is unlikely to operate when the vehicle runs forward in going down a hill. Failure for the breeching to work will mean that the cart continues to run forward, so the tugs go further forward and the back band pushes the saddle forward towards the horse's withers. The belly band will go forward towards the elbows and will be likely to chafe. Worse still, the crupper back strap will be tightened and the horse will be forced to take the weight of the vehicle on his dock via his crupper. This is very likely to lead to kicking or, at the least, an extremely sore tail. If, on the other hand, the breeching is too tight, the horse's quarters will soon become chafed. The horse must neither be jammed into the vehicle, between his collar and breeching, like a straight jacket, nor put to, so loosely, that the vehicle runs a great distance backwards and forwards, in changing from uphill to downhill and vice versa. For instance, in going over a hump-back bridge, the pull and push should be taken gently as the pressure changes from shoulders to quarters and back again. A final check must be made to see that the belly band is neither too tight nor too loose as explained previously.

When the horse is standing up into his collar, with the traces taut, the shaft tips should be about level with the hames. Shafts which are too short can get caught under the collar and can also dig into the animal's shoulders. Shafts which are too long, in front of the tug stop, can

38 *A movable foot-rest on a Dog Cart.*

catch the reins and can also dig into the horse's neck during tight turns. There should be enough distance between the horse's quarters and the dashboard to enable the animal to carry his tail comfortably. The dashboard must be well away from the quarters in descending hills when the breeching comes into action. Horses with high tail carriages, such as Arabians, need more room and will be very uncomfortable if they cannot hold up their tails.

The height of the shafts in the tugs, assuming that the vehicle fits correctly, can be seen by the level of the seat. The seat needs to be at the horizontal in order to give the driver and passenger a comfortable ride. It is essential that all seat cushions are strapped to the vehicle; loose cushions are dangerous. Should a horse stumble, or do anything violent, there is a grave possibility of the cushion falling from the seat and the driver and passenger may get thrown onto the road. If a movable foot rest is used, it is very important to ensure that it is secured firmly to the floor of the vehicle.

Mounting

Before mounting the carriage it is wise to walk right round for a final check to see that all is well. On no account should a passenger mount before the driver, or Whip, as he or she is called. If a passenger were to mount and the horse become frightened and take off, the passenger would be powerless to do anything. In fact, at no time must there be a passenger in the vehicle without the driver being in position on the box seat. It is usual for the whip to be put into the whip socket, before mounting. Some people prefer to mount with the whip in their hand, saying that if the horse steps back, they can send him forward with the whip. The danger is, particularly with novices, of the horse becoming inadvertently touched with the whip as the driver mounts. Some whip holders are fixed onto the dashboard which means that the whip gets in the way of mounting on that side. This prevents the reins from being handled correctly. A few coach builders put the whip socket on the floor so that the whip slopes from the dashboard across to the seat, at the entrance to the carriage. This, again, is a nuisance. The best place for the whip holder is on the rail or body of the carriage to the right of the driver's seat so that the whip can rest there, out of harm's way, whilst putting to and mounting.

If rugs are being used, these can be folded and placed on the seats, ready for use, or hung over the seat back. If a driving apron is worn, then it is best to tuck one side of this up into the waistband, rather in the same way that a side-saddle rider does with her skirt when she is dismounted. Thus the apron is kept out of the way when getting into the carriage. It is otherwise possible to stand on the apron when one foot is on the step of the vehicle, whilst attempting to mount. If this happens, mounting is effectively prevented. If mounting from the offside, the reins are pulled out from the offside terret and taken in the left hand, in the driving position, with the nearside rein on top of the offside rein and the splices level. The nearside rein lies over the top of the index finger and the offside rein lies below the middle finger. The end of the reins is put over the right arm, in order to keep them off the ground and away from the steps when the time comes to mount. The right hand is now placed in front of the left and the nearside rein is put under the index finger and the offside rein below the third finger.

39 *Preparing to mount.*

Tension can then be taken, on the reins, between the two hands, without pressure being put accidentally onto the animal's mouth as the Whip steps back towards the mounting step. The left hand can now let go of the reins which are held firmly in the right, with the fingers gripping them to prevent them from slipping if the horse should try to move forward. The mounting handle can be held between the fore finger and thumb of the right hand and control can be maintained over the horse with the reins held securely in this way. The left hand is used on the left mounting handle. The Whip should mount quickly and quietly and sit down as soon as possible. The reins are now transferred back to the left hand and the fact that the splices were level, prior to mounting, will ensure that if the horse should step forward an even pull is taken. If a knee rug is used, instead of an apron, this can now be tucked round the driver. The whip is taken from the socket by the right hand and held, at the point of balance, near the top ferrule. The right hand is then placed on the reins, in front of the left, in the position in which it was before mounting.

Once the driver is in full control of the horse, the passengers may then mount. If the driver wishes to mount from the nearside, this is quite acceptable. The principle of mounting is the same but the obvious changes must be made, for example, the reins are held in the left hand when mounting. Care must be taken not to take too much contact on the animal's mouth throughout the mounting procedure. This can result in the horse stepping back because he misunderstands the wishes of his driver who is, unwittingly, asking him to rein back. Also, of course, the reins must not be too long as the driver would initially have no control.

Position on the box

The position of the driver, or Whip, on the box seat is important. It is very difficult to drive properly and safely if the seat is the wrong height to allow comfortable purchase for the feet. If the seat is too high, and the floor cannot be reached properly with the feet, the Whip will be unable to check the horse if he should start to pull hard. If the animal stumbles, the driver might even be pulled off the seat. It will be found that, even with a quiet horse, lack of purchase by the driver's or passenger's feet, over rough ground, can create back problems as any jarring is taken entirely on the spine. The most comfortable position, for the Whip, is that which is obtained by using a sloping box seat as was used on such vehicles as Road Coaches, Private Drags and Dog Carts well over a century ago. Many modern carriage builders are now making such box seats as the demand has increased.

40 *A box seat on a Dog Cart.*

When using a sloping seat, the Whip is able to sit with a reasonably straight thigh and lower leg. The feet can rest, either on the upward sloping floor of the vehicle, or a foot rest. Some vehicles have a rest, which can be moved forwards or backwards, as desired, to suit varying lengths of leg. This position enables good purchase for control over the horse, if he should pull. It allows the legs, back and shoulders to be used as well as the arms and hands if the need arises. This is far more effective than the position provided by a low seat which forces the driver to sit with his legs bent back. It affords very little purchase against a pulling animal and is extremely uncomfortable. It can often cause an aching back and stiff shoulders and makes the driver resemble a certain type of garden gnome.

Care, however, must be taken when putting a high box or padded cushion onto a seat to ensure that the side and back rails are high enough to prevent the driver from being thrown out of the carriage if a severe bump is encountered. It is important to sit squarely on the box seat, with the hips and shoulders straight and the head held high. Nothing looks worse than the sight of a Whip, or groom, sitting with his or her legs apart and bent at the knees. Rounded shoulders, outstretched arms, a rein in each hand and the whip in the socket, immediately ruin the overall appearance of the smartest horse and carriage. On the other hand, the general impression which is given by a straight-backed Whip, sitting on a sloping box with knees together and feet firmly on the floor or foot rest, and reins and whip held correctly, is one of elegance, confidence and expertise.

The use and choice of a whip

No attempt should ever be made to drive without a whip in the right hand. It is an essential aid which can be used in order to help to convey the wishes of the driver to the horse or horses. A rider has the use of his voice, hands, legs and seat. A driver cannot use legs or seat and so a whip is an essential additional aid. The driving whip is never used severely; indeed, it is unsuitably constructed for that. The thong and lash is just drawn across the horse either between the collar and the saddle or immediately behind the saddle, as a back up to the voice to tell the horse to go forward. It should be used as a training aid which can be applied if the horse neglects to obey the voice alone. Of course there are times when the whip might be used to prevent a horse from evading his driver, such as by stepping sideways or backwards. With a well-trained horse, the thong can be hung alongside the horse's ribs to hold him to one side in the way that a rider's leg would.

A driving whip which is suitable for everyday use can be bought quite cheaply. It is important to choose one which is comfortable to hold. The length of the stick, and the thong, relate to the equipage with which it will be used. One which is too short will not be satisfactory as it will be impossible to reach the horse in the desired place without extending the right arm a long way forward. Equally, a whip which either has too long a stick or too long a thong will be a nuisance as the horse may get touched inadvertently.

Traditional whips for private driving and coaching were, and still are, often made of holly. A really good holly whip should lie lightly in the hand. The fine thong, with an even finer lash at the end, will be exactly the right length to reach the single horse or, in the case of a pair, either horse. Whips made for tandem are longer, with longer thongs and those for team – so that the near leader can be reached – even longer. The skill of a coachman to touch the near leader, by his pad, with his whip, without contacting any of the other three horses, is the origin of the word 'Whip' in referring to a driver. A good holly whip will be expensive to buy and great care has to be taken of it. It is easily broken and could be hard to replace. Such a whip must *never ever* be used for long-reining or lungeing, however tempting it may seem, for convenience, at the time; such use nearly always results in it getting broken.

93

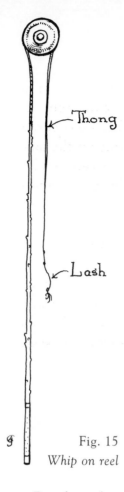

Thong

Lash

Fig. 15
Whip on reel

Holly whips are best saved purely for the high days of driving. When the whip is not in use, it should be kept hanging on a whip reel and never be left lying in a corner where the stick is almost certain to acquire a bend. Once it is out of true, it will not be as pleasant to handle and use. It must never be hung on a nail, by its thong, as this will soon develop a sharp bend. The whip reel should be fixed to a wall, about seven feet from the ground. It is made of wood with a groove around its circumference into which the thong, near the top, is put. This holds the whip off the floor and helps to develop the top of the thong into a shepherd's crook shape. Then, when the whip is used, the thong hangs neatly from the stick. When the whip is being taken to a show, it should be put onto a board with a reel or similar, round-shaped, block at the end. The thong is put round the reel and the stick is secured along the board.

Some holly whips are made with a central joint enabling them to be carried on a board, on the back of a team vehicle such as a Break or Coach, in case the whip which is being used gets broken. The trouble with a jointed whip is that the metal fitting, halfway along the stick, tends to affect the balance adversely.

Dog-leg whips are favoured by some people. The dog-leg shaped bend, which was created by the growth of the holly stick, is said to prevent rain from dripping down the stick into the driver's sleeve. Everyday whips are often made of nylon and other modern materials. They are quite adequate for driving at home and for cross-country events. Some are made in a similar way to a light lungeing whip. The ones to be avoided are those which have thick handles and, when held, appear to weigh heavily in the hand dragging the right wrist down in the process. Such a whip will make the right arm ache and will be very wearying to hold for any length of time. When purchasing a whip, it is best to take the whip in the right hand, and hold both hands in front of the body, in the driving position, as if on the reins, to see if it feels comfortable. If it feels heavy, then leave it where it is.

Handling the reins

Before attempting to drive a horse, it is a good idea to set up some kind of driving apparatus on which to practise the handling of the reins. In this way the newcomer to driving can see for himself, as weights rise and fall, exactly how much pressure he would be putting on the animal's mouth. It very often surprises beginners and even people who have driven for some years, when they see how a slight turn or alteration of the position of the wrist can increase and decrease the contact on the horse's mouth so much.

Sophisticated weights and pulleys can be made. With these, cord is used to lie over each pulley. A weight of about six hundred and twenty grams (one pound and six ounces) is fixed to one end of the cord and a rein to the other end. The two pulleys are then temporarily clamped to an object, such as a kitchen table, and the pupil can practise the rein handling whenever there is time to spare. A simple apparatus can be set

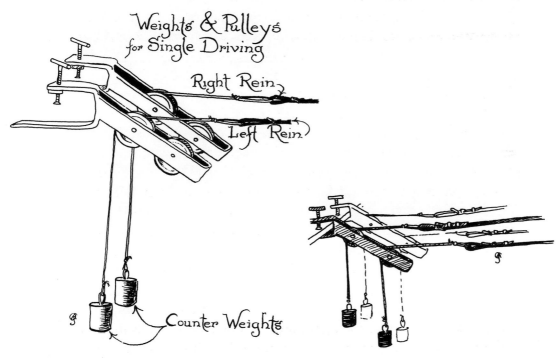

Fig. 16a *Driving weights and pulleys*

Fig. 16b *Driving weights and pulleys for tandem etc.*

up using two rings, two bits of rope, two dog leads and four horseshoes. The rings can be tied to a rail, about fifteen centimetres (six inches) apart. A piece of rope is passed through each ring with the two horseshoes, to make over four hundred and fifty grams (one pound) for each

41 *The hands, working in unison.*

rein, tied to one end and two dog leads, for reins, are fastened to the other ends.

It is essential, when learning to drive, that the traditional rein handling is learned and practised. This is the A B C to all future driving. Some people mistakenly refer to the traditional British style as 'one-handed' driving. They claim that they would never be able to control their animal with only their left hand. This has, understandably, led to some confusion. The traditional method is not 'one handed': both hands are used, working in unison. The reins are anchored in the left hand and the right hand is placed over the reins in front of the left hand so the horse is controlled by both hands. Once the method is understood it will be found that it forms a solid foundation for all that follows. If the beginner perseveres with this method, in the early stages, although it may appear to be difficult, he or she will almost certainly become a far more accomplished Whip than the person who has taken short cuts and failed to establish this correct grounding. This handling will allow pair, tandem, team, unicorn and random to follow with little worry or trouble. Once the traditional method has been established, then it is quite all right to adopt differing rein handling, as desired, for scurry and trials driving where other methods have their place and are quite acceptable.

The main reason for not separating the reins, for all driving (i.e. a rein in each hand), is that shortening the reins takes longer and that it is impossible to use the whip at the same time as keeping the horse straight. As the right hand goes forward to apply the whip, so the contact with the right side of his mouth is lost.

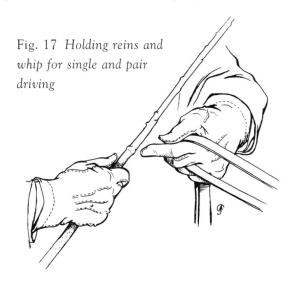

Fig. 17 *Holding reins and whip for single and pair driving*

Having set up the weights and pulleys it is now a good idea for the pupil to see for himself how the right side of the horse's mouth gets dropped if the reins are held in two separated hands as the whip is used.

For this proof, it is simplest to take the left rein in the left hand and the right rein in the right hand, as in riding. Contact now has to be made on the animal's mouth so the reins must be pulled until the weights rise and both are level. A wooden spoon can be held in the right hand, to represent the whip, alongside the rein. Now, pretend to hit the horse with the spoon, whilst holding the right rein, and it will be seen how the right weight drops considerably. Assuming that he were being driven with contact, this would send him veering away to the left very smartly. So, the reins must now be taken in the traditional rein-handling method which has been used by generations of coachmen who were experts at their job.

Dealing first with the left hand: it is essential to keep the wrist at the correct angle. The hand is held about three inches in front of the centre of the body. The wrist should be light, strong, supple and rounded. The angle of the hand is so that the knuckles face towards the horse. The thumb lies straight across the top of the hand, from left to right. It neither sticks up nor points down. Both reins are secured in this, the anchor hand. The nearside (left) rein lies over the index finger and the offside (right) rein lies under the middle finger. Having both reins lying on top of each other, down through the palm of the hand, the little finger followed by the others can close down on the reins to prevent them from slipping. Now, take a pull and make sure

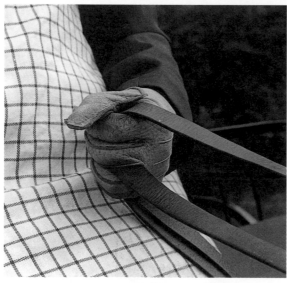

42 *The reins in the left hand.*

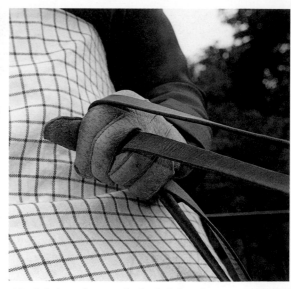

43 *A left incline with the left hand.*

44 *A right incline with the left hand.*

that both weights are level and the hand is still remaining in what I call the 'neutral' position. The pulley 'horse' will be proceeding in a straight line, with even contact on both sides of his mouth. Next try an incline to the left with just the left hand. The purpose of this is to prove how much contact is increased by a turn of the wrist. In order to do this, turn the wrist so that the knuckles face uppermost. This shortens the left rein considerably, putting pressure onto the nearside of the horse's mouth and it loosens the contact on the offside which allows the horse to bend through the incline. Go back to the 'neutral' position of the wrist and make sure that the weights are level. Keep practising this left incline until the position is familiar and the left weight rises and falls easily and smoothly.

The incline to the right with just the left hand on both reins is more difficult. The left hand is rotated in the opposite direction so that the palm is facing uppermost. This can be likened to looking at the time as a pocket watch lies in the palm of the left hand. Except, on this occasion the fingers are kept closed on the reins to prevent them from slipping. It will be noticed that the left rein lengthens and the left weight will fall. The right weight will rise a little. Providing that there is contact on the animal's mouth this will loosen the left side as it increases pressure on the right and a well-schooled light-mouthed, animal will come round to the right. This right incline is always found to be more difficult than the left, at this stage.

Beginners to driving, who have ridden, very often swing their hands to the side from which an animal is shying, to hold him towards the object. This works well in riding but has the opposite effect when driving. So, if a one-handed incline has to be made to the right, the left hand is turned to the 'pocket watch' angle, to lengthen the left rein, and as increased pressure is needed on the right rein, the left hand is drawn

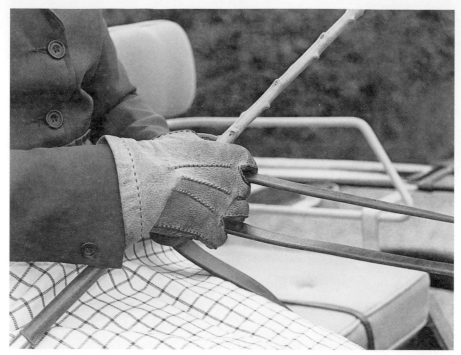

45 *The right hand in position with two fingers separating the reins.*

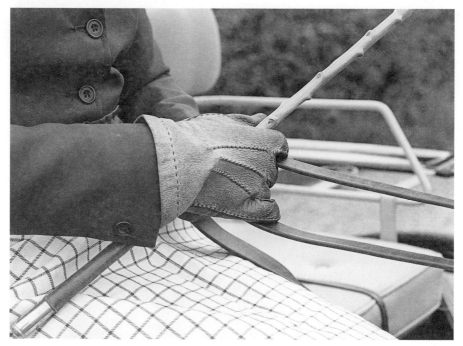

46 *The right hand in position with three fingers separating the reins.*

back and held towards the left hip. This is very effective in shortening the right rein. One occasion when this might be necessary is at a road junction when the whip is being held to the right to signal to people behind of the intention to turn right. This incline needs to be made purely with the left hand. Another time is for driving a one-handed circle, which can be thought of as purely an incline which is maintained, in a dressage arena, at advanced level, and applies particularly with the handling of a pair. Care has to be taken to shorten the reins before such a one-handed incline is being made. Otherwise it will be found that the hand gets too near to the body for it to be effective.

Having thoroughly established the inclines to the left and right with just the left hand, the right hand is now brought into position on both reins. It is safest and most workmanlike to keep the right hand in front of the left, on both reins all the time. It is then in position to work in unison with the left, assisting in turns to the left and right and in steadying the horse and in pulling up. The angle of the right hand is similar to that of the left. As with the left wrist, there should be no stiffness. The wooden spoon (representing the whip) is held lightly, under the thumb muscle, between the thumb and fore finger. The right hand is held on the reins, a couple of inches in front of the left hand. The forefinger lies over the nearside rein and either the three remaining fingers or the second and third fingers, depending on personal preference, lie over the offside rein. Contact can now be taken on the weights with both hands and experimental evidence will prove how comfortable this will feel. The hands will learn to work together and the result will be a much happier, steadier horse if an even contact is maintained on his mouth. Make sure that the weights are level and that both wrists are supple and rounded with the knuckles facing forward, towards the horse. A turn to the left should be made with the hands working in unison. The left wrist turns, as previously practised, to increase the contact on the left rein and slacken the contact on the right rein. Additional pressure on the left rein can easily be applied by the fingers of the right hand on the underside of the left rein, in front of the left hand. If a stronger aid is needed then the right hand can be placed, with the knuckles uppermost, over the left rein just in front of the left hand and pressure applied. The method to be chosen depends on preference and on the lightness and obedience of the horse and the severity of the turn. A close watch on the weights will reveal what is happening. If

47 *A left turn with the right hand under the left rein.*

48 *A left turn with the right hand over the left rein.*

both weights rise upwards with the left weight going up more, then the poor pulley 'horse' is being told to stop as well as turn to the left. So, the hands must be sorted out until pressure is being put where it is needed, purely on the left rein as the right rein slackens slightly to allow the horse to bend through the turn.

When a right turn is needed, the left hand goes into the 'pocket watch' angle to loosen the left rein as the right hand is placed, with the back of the hand uppermost, over the offside rein to apply the necessary amount of pressure to bring the horse round. On no account should the right hand be brought to the right which will cause a loop of slack rein to hang between the hands. Care must be taken to ensure that the right-hand index finger does not remain pressing on top of the left rein when asking for a right turn. It is a common fault with beginners who then cannot understand why the horse is not responding to their request to turn right. A close watch on the weights will reveal such mistakes.

During these practice sessions, it is essential to hold a wooden spoon or a stick of some kind, in the right hand. Failure to do this will almost certainly result in the right thumb creeping under the reins and the right wrist will go to the wrong angle, with a tendency to become stiff and hollow instead of soft and rounded. The 'whip' must be held at forty-five degrees, or ten or twelve, in

49 *A right turn with the right hand over the right rein.*

relation to the reins. This is the most comfortable angle to put the right hand into the desired soft position. When the whip is used, it is essential to take the right hand off the reins. The lash should be placed well forward on the horse, in the area around the saddle and *never* on the quarters.

Shortening the reins is achieved by sliding the right hand up the reins, a few inches, towards the horse. The left hand comes up behind the right and the reins are shortened. The left hand must *never* be taken off the reins for shortening, like a sailor climbing up a rope. It is a bad habit to develop at this stage. The reason is that if and when the newcomer progresses to driving tandem, team or random, taking the left hand off four or six reins could prove disastrous. It can take a very long time to get the fingers back into the desired position between the reins once they have been moved. Drama may follow because the hand was, presumably, moved at the start of some trouble.

Although the method of traditional rein handling may sound difficult, it is, in fact, very simple. Once it is learned and practised, it will become second nature. All subsequent methods can then be tried and used when desired and the correct traditional handling will remain firmly as a foundation. Sensitive hands, which are light and yet strong, are essential for driving. The Whip has only his hands, voice and whip as aids, unlike a rider who also has his seat and legs. It is essential that the handling of the reins is practised, away from the horse, until it becomes as perfect as possible. Failure to understand how turns of the wrist alter the contact on the animal's mouth is the cause of a lot of problems. This is why it is so helpful to spend time studying the weights on pulleys, in relation to the angle of the hands. It saves a tremendous amount of discomfort to the horse if the problems can be put right on an inanimate object instead of the sensitive mouth of a long-suffering animal. Once the method is thoroughly understood, then the best thing to do is to get up behind a horse, accompanied by an experienced driving person, and drive as much as possible. From this point on, it is sheer mileage which makes a competent driver.

Going for a drive including the balancing of a two-wheeled vehicle

Once the driver has mounted and given the command to the horse to 'walk-on', the hands must give to allow the animal to lean into his collar to move the vehicle forward. If, when the horse tries to walk forward, he is met with a dead, unyielding, feel on his mouth, he may wonder whether he is meant to stop or go. This could result in him stepping back instead of forward, or plunging or even rearing, in extreme cases. The hands should follow through the movement and just give a little, without dropping the contact, as he walks forward. If he hesitates, he should be asked again to 'walk-on'. He should not be hit on the loins with the reins as this will almost certainly cause him to leap forward in fright. He must not be jabbed in the mouth, as an aid to go forward, as this is likely to have the reverse effect. Newcomers to driving, who are riders, are inclined to sit forward and try to urge the horse on with their seat and legs, from the vehicle. This ineffective habit must not develop. If the horse does not walk on, the whip can be drawn across his back, in the area by the saddle, as far forward as possible. It is not wise to use the whip on the hindquarters. This could cause kicking. It is quite possible to get kicked through the dashboard. A steel-shod hoof penetrating a dashboard and coming into contact with a driver's shin is not to be recommended. It can, and does, happen and is a very unpleasant experience.

The secret of good driving is to sit up straight and be appearing to do very little. Light and sympathetic, yet positive hands will usually produce a responsive horse. This does not mean leaving the horse on a loose rein, with no contact, which will make him wonder what he is meant to be doing and where he is meant to be going. Expert drivers will usually be seen to keep their hands very still and yet the horse will be doing all that is required with little apparent effort from the driver.

Once the horse is walking forward quietly, from the halt, he should be driven for the first half mile, or so, at the walk. Very often this pace is neglected. It is important to spend time working on the horse's walk. He should move freely forward, with the hooves hitting the ground with a regular four-time beat. Many horses walk in a rhythm which is

105

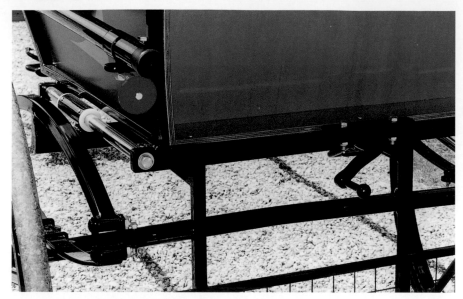

50 *The rear view of a Bennington Back Step Buggy to show how the balance is altered by turning the handle.*

so hurried that it is more inclined to two-time than four-time, with the hoof beats neither regular nor even. The horse should be encouraged to walk with a long stride. It is interesting to lean over the side of the vehicle and note where the horse is putting his feet. Ideally, with a free, onward going walk the hind foot should go beyond the mark that the front foot, on the same side, has, or would have, made. If the horse is not tracking up with his hind foot, then he should be driven on to lengthen his stride and made to use his hindquarters more. Driving at a sloppy and slow walk is not a good practice and can result in stumbling or worse still, falling.

Whilst the horse is walking, the harness can be noted for correct adjustment. If the tugs are not resting against the tug stops or the breeching appears to be too tight or too loose, then it is best to pull up and put things right. If harness has to be adjusted, be sure to get the passenger out of the vehicle to hold the horse. The balance of a two-wheeled vehicle should be checked. This is frequently altered by varying weights of passengers so may need adjusting. The shafts should be seen almost to float in the tugs. The tug-buckle points will, ideally, chatter against the tug buckles. There should neither be weight on the horse's back nor on his belly. If the shafts are bearing down on his back, he will be having to carry part of the carriage, as well as pull it. This, as well as making the work unnecessarily hard for the horse, is likely to result in a sore back. If the shafts are tipping upwards, because there is too much weight on the back of the vehicle, the horse will have pressure on his girth area as the belly band is being pulled upwards. He will be made extremely uncomfortable.

As well as an unbalanced vehicle causing discomfort to the horse, it can cause breakages to the vehicle. Many modern carriages are made with metal shafts. The stress of a badly balanced vehicle can cause metal fatigue at the point where the shafts are fixed near the front of the vehicle. This can result in broken shafts and a horrible accident. The same can, of course, apply to wooden shafts but generally there is more warning, as the paint shows cracks when the wood begins to develop a shake or split. Metal fatigues rather more silently under the paint and can suddenly give way without any warning.

There are various methods of balancing two-wheeled vehicles. Some modern carriages are built with sophisticated mechanisms by which the vehicle body is moved forwards and backwards, relative to the axle, to obtain the desired balance, by means of a handle at the back which is turned. A similar principle was employed, over a century ago, on some high Dog Carts which were used for tandem driving so that the balance could be adjusted according to whether the groom was carried on the rear seat, or alongside the Whip.

Traditional vehicles such as Ralli Cars and Country Carts have varying methods for altering the positions of the seats. The most usual is that the seat is on runners and its position is altered, forwards or backwards, by means of a central handle. This is given a half turn to release a rod which fits into slots on the runners enabling the seat to be moved. Some have a slot running fore and aft in the centre of the seat. There is a bolt which drops down through this to a structure below, to hold the seat into the desired place. It is secured with a wing nut or similar fixing. The systems are many and varied. The principle remains the same in that the front seat can be moved forwards or backwards as desired.

With a two-wheeled vehicle which has back to back seats, it will be found that it is usually only possible to carry very light people on the rear-facing back seats. If too much weight is put on the rear seats, the front seat has to be pulled so far forward, to compensate the rear weight,

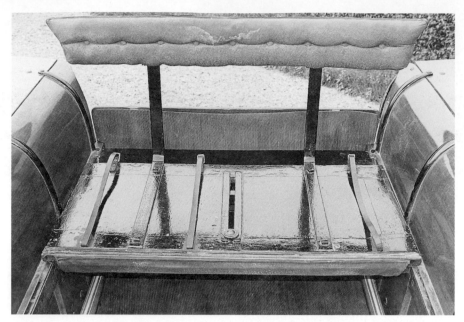

51 *A nineteenth-century Ralli Car with adjustment for balance made by a bolt on the centre of the seat. Here the seat is pushed back to balance the vehicle for the driver and one passenger on the front seat. The seat cushion is removed for clarity.*

that the driver is forced to try to drive with his legs bent right under him. If more than two people are frequently carried it is better to use a four-wheeled vehicle like a Waggonette or a Four-Wheeled Dog Cart, so that the rear-seat passengers can be accommodated in comfort. The only significance then, of their weight, is that it is more for the horse to pull.

Governess Carts are balanced by the positioning of the occupants. The driver sits in the rear right-hand corner and it is up to the passengers to sit in whichever position results in the correct balance of the vehicle. Gigs usually have fixed seats so the balance has to have been correct when the vehicle was made. Varying weights of driver and passenger can affect this balance and it is sometimes necessary for the passenger to alter his position on the seat to keep the balance to the desired place. The Whip should sit in the position from which he finds it most comfortable to drive. Some carriages can be troublesome to balance and it may be found that if a weight is carried on the floor, or hung in the back, this can be placed into the position which makes the vehicle balance correctly. Once this is discovered, then it might be a

52 *The same Ralli Car with the seat pushed forward to balance the vehicle when one or two light passengers are carried on the rear facing seat.*

good idea to get a carriage builder to add a lead weight to achieve the same effect. Too tight a belly band can make the vehicle appear as if the balance is wrong. Such restriction to the shafts can cause the vehicle to shake with every stride that the horse makes. This gives a motion to the driver and passenger which is known as 'knee rock'.

Once a check has been made that all is well and the horse has settled into a free forward walk, he can be asked to 'trot on' in the same way that he was asked to 'walk on' from the halt. Before giving words of command it is important to get the horse's attention by calling his name. It is very often best to give all onward going commands with sharp, two-syllable words like 'trot on', 'walk on', 'go on', 'get on' etc. and all slowing down words with a slower type of word in a long single syllable like 'walk', 'trot', 'whoa', said slowly and drawn out. It is not good to click to get the animal to go on because one person's click can sound very similar, to the horse, to another person's click. One day, someone may click and the horse will leap forward, thinking that he was meant to go on. The driver of the horse is likely not to have heard the click and to be taken by surprise; an accident may follow. If upward gradients have to be negotiated, it is easier for the horse to pull his load, in terms of light carriage, up the hill at a trot. The exception to this is obviously with heavy loads when the horse is reduced to a walk by the sheer weight and strain. This is unlikely to be found with private driving carriages in normal conditions. It is best to walk down hills. Trotting down a hill could result in the horse being pushed off his feet and end in a fall and broken knees.

If slippery roads are a problem, it may be a good idea to have hardened nails or studs put in the shoes when the horse is shod. A couple of nails which have hardened centres, used on the outer sides of the hind shoes, can be a great help to give purchase against slipping and also help to save wear. Some people use studs on the heels of the front shoes to prevent slipping whilst others, including Bert Barley, in London in the nineteen forties, would not hear of their use. He maintained that the concussion caused by prevention of the front feet sliding a little at every stride, on London's hard roads, played havoc with the working horse's legs. A calkin on the outer hind heel of both hind shoes is also a great help to prevent slipping on grassy surfaces. Shoes with these have compensating wedge heels. Harness horses can work well in fullered, concave, hunter shoes. It is not necessary to use heavy flat shoes for private driving. Some people prefer these heavy shoes to get more action from their animals. It is, however, possible to create foot problems with heavy shoes and they have even been known to be the cause of laminitis. If roads are slippery, it is a wise precaution to drive in the exercise type of knee pads. When the horse is driven round a corner, it is sensible to steady the pace and keep him well balanced. If he is driven too fast, when cornering, he could lose his balance and go down on his side.

The pace, at the trot, on the level, should be kept to a steady rhythm. The horse must not be allowed, or made, to go everywhere at a fast trot. This will not do his legs much good. He should be driven at a pace which takes a minimum of effort on his part. The speed will vary from about five to nine miles per hour depending on the size of the animal and the length of his stride. It is quite surprising how many miles can be covered at this steady pace, with little trouble.

The last mile should be driven at the walk, in order to cool the horse off before he is taken back to his stable or field. This is usually a good time to school the horse to walk freely with a long stride. He will probably be keen to get home and, with luck, will swing along using his hindquarters correctly and overtrack his front foot marks with his hind feet. From the point of view of the Whip, and his rein handling, it is trouble-free mileage which develops confidence and competence. Daily drives will help to build up a rapport between the horse and his driver.

Dress

The main considerations for dress, worn by the Whip, are practicality and neatness. As far as lady Whips are concerned, large-brimmed hats, lace gloves, high-heeled shoes, and tight short skirts must be avoided. Large rings on the fingers and ears are also a mistake. For everyday driving, a small hat keeps the hair from the eyes and, if the weather is cold, keeps the Whip warmer than if he or she were to drive hatless. It is also considered to be more correct. Most drivers wear hard hats for cross-country competitions. It is sensible to wear such hats for everyday driving.

In the show ring, gentlemen Whips, when driving a town vehicle or gig, can wear a top hat if the occasion is dressy; otherwise a bowler hat is correct. For informal occasions, such as meets and country drives, a cloth cap or other soft hat is acceptable if a hard hat is not being worn. Lady Whips are advised to wear a well-fitting, small-brimmed hat in the show ring. Wearing a wide-brimmed hat is disastrous: a high wind, a pulling horse and a salute to the occupants of the Royal Box can become a nightmare for the wearer of such a creation. A coat and skirt and toning blouse can be worn in the show ring. Trousers are acceptable for ladies at driving Meets and for cross-country events. Gentlemen can wear suits for smart occasions and jackets and slacks for country driving. Shoes, for all, are best if they have rubber soles as leather can both slip and scratch the paint. Polished leather shoes are ideal for showing, whilst shoes such as trainers can ruin an otherwise very smart turn-out. Of course, for ladies, high-heeled shoes are dangerous as they can get caught in the step when mounting or dismounting. Gloves are essential to protect the fingers from the reins if the horse should pull hard and should, ideally, be of unlined leather. Those which are one size too large will be found to be more comfortable than those which fit exactly. It is a good idea to have a spare pair of string gloves in case of rain when reins can become slippery in leather gloves.

Large ornamental rings should be avoided because they can dig into the fingers and cause quite a lot of pain; ear rings can get caught in branches of trees, so should not be worn when going across country. The traditional flower of the British Driving Society is the yellow carnation, so, if the occasion is dressy and a button hole is worn, it can be this. Members of the Coaching Club wear the cornflower as their button hole. An apron is worn (by the Whip and social passengers but not by grooms) to protect the clothes from the grease and hairs from the reins and horse and is correct for showing. It is in order to use a rug in preference to an apron for the same purpose. For cold-weather driving this is preferable, as it keeps the occupants a lot warmer. Reversible rugs and aprons which have waterproof material on one side and wool on the other are suitable for cold weather whilst those made of check material are ideal for summer use. At the beginning of the nineteen hundreds, lavish, fur-lined, rugs were used, through the winter, to keep the occupants of the coachman-driven family carriage, such as a Landau or Omnibus, warm. In those days, copper foot and hand warmers were filled with boiling water for the same purpose.

Transporting a turn-out

Once it is decided to attend rallies or competitions then it is necessary to consider how the horse, carriage and all that goes with it are to be transported. The simplest method is to load everything into a horse box. Some are beautifully equipped for the horse and carriage and have sophisticated living accommodation enabling competitors who spend a large proportion of the season away, to have some of the comforts of home. Everything is loaded and kept under one cover. Many now have superb portable stabling which can be erected alongside the box.

At the other end of the scale is the person who attends just a few shows and club events. One simple way of combining a shopping car with part of the transport is to have a four-wheel drive pick-up truck. The carriage can be winched up ramps and will ride in the truck. The shafts lie over a ladder rack, behind the top of the cab, being padded and tied down. The hand turned winch, behind the cab, holds the vehicle forward. A rope on each side of the carriage axle, by the sides

53 *A vehicle being loaded onto a Land Rover.*

54 *The Land Rover and trailer which was used by the author in the nineteen eighties.*

55 *The horsebox which was built to specification for the author to carry her two ponies and vehicle.*

of the hubs, prevents the vehicle from running forward. The ramps are carried on the floor of the truck. The trailer is then hitched and one driver can transport the equipage using one towing vehicle. Another method which takes two drivers and two motor vehicles is to use a carriage trailer behind one car and the horse trailer behind another car. This is expensive as running costs are doubled.

If only one small pony is being taken around, then it is possible to get both the pony and the carriage into a horse trailer. Care should be taken to keep the two separated because of damage to either. It is best to have a movable partition so that the vehicle can be kept quite separately. If the pony is loaded first, a trailer with a front ramp as well as a rear ramp should be used. If there were to be a road emergency and there was need to get the pony out in a hurry, there might not be time to untie and get the vehicle out first. In case of a fire, the pony could be burned to death. It is usually best to have the vehicle at the back because the shafts can be left over the rear ramp to give more room. Take care, though, not to reverse into a wall, once the cart is loaded. This has been done. Some large, long, double-ramped trailers are made which will accommodate a pair of horses and a four-wheeled vehicle. Ideas are best gained by walking around the horse-box parking area at a horse driving trials or driving show.

Driving in company

Before taking a horse out in company to a show, or even a rally, it is wise to take him out with other animals in quiet and familiar surroundings. Horses in blinkers can be afraid when they hear the presence of another animal in harness until they get used to the idea. It is best to go out with just one other turn-out to begin with. First, drive behind and be sure to tell the person who is helping to keep looking back to see that all is well. If the young horse gets upset, it may be better to let him go in front. When the track is wide enough, the leading horse can slow down or halt and the other one can overtake and vice versa. Eventually, when confidence is gained, the two can be driven side by side when both animals are able to hear but, because of blinkers, cannot see each other. This is often the most bewildering position for the inexperienced horse. Attention paid to this apparently small detail will make all the

56 *British Driving Society members at a Meet at Ickworth Park in Suffolk. Mr Fred and Miss Margaret Collins are in the foreground with their Shetland pony, Nellie, to a Governess Cart.*

difference when it comes to driving in company at a rally or show.

When the beginner attends his first rally it is a good idea to arrive in plenty of time before the drive is due to depart. The horse can then be given time to settle after his journey in the horse box. He can be unboxed, harnessed and put to at leisure. It is when this has to be done in a hurry, often surrounded by friends who are chattering, that mistakes are made and accidents caused. If the animal is on edge, it may be a help to walk him about in his harness before putting to. It is best to add a lunge line, at a time like this, for safety. For this purpose it is threaded through the nearside of the bit and over the top of the head before being buckled to the offside of the bit. This gives very strong control as it works rather like a gag bit. It can lie quite loosely but is there in case of emergency. It will give the handler more control if the horse should turn and wrap himself up in the reins. Ideally, of course, if serious long reining is planned, the proper long reins, rather than the shorter driving reins, must be used because of the danger of the handler getting kicked. When the driver and horse are happy, the horse can be put to and walked quietly about whilst other people are getting ready. This gives time to check that the harness and balance is correctly adjusted before the drive moves off.

The best place, in a convoy of turn-outs, is right behind the person who is leading the drive. The drive organiser should be told that this is the newcomer's first rally and they will almost certainly keep a watchful eye. It is essential to carry an active passenger who will be able to help if there is trouble.

Driving people in general are kind to one another. If anyone needs help, it is usual for everyone to pull up and wait whilst the difficulty is put right. Each person is fully aware that it could be them on the next occasion who is the cause of a hold up. It is wise to carry a spares kit of some sort in the boot of the vehicle. The essentials are a length of strong cord and a sharp knife. A mobile phone is a good idea as is pencil and paper for leaving a message and a head collar and rope in case the horse has to be taken from the vehicle and tied up. Other useful items are a leather punch, spare trace and rein, spare hame strap and first-aid equipment for both horse and human. The list is endless and it can be great fun making up a spares box with all kinds of contents from sets of shoes and blacksmith's tools to shaft splices, jubilee clips and wheel wrenches.

It is sensible to take the animal to a few rallies and non-competitive fixtures before embarking on a show or event. The addition of the pressures of competition can cause a lot of nervousness to the Whip, grooms and passengers. This is immediately transmitted to the horse who may then become nervous too. It is for this reason that the author uses an equine aromatic called Pax which is obtainable from Day, Son and Hewitt of St George's Quay, Lancaster, LAI 5QJ. She believes, and has repeatedly proved, that a little Pax rubbed onto the hands and forehead smother the aroma of adrenalin which is apparently given off at times of excitement, created by nature's way of putting the body into top gear. It does not have to come from the handler but can come, just as well, from passengers and other competitors. This theory is fully described in *Breaking a Horse to Harness*, so will not be repeated here.

Showing

57 *Mrs Chris Dick driving Mr and Mrs S. Murrell's Hackney, Wentworth Prince Regent, to a Round Backed Gig. Winners of numerous private driving championships.*

It is best for a newcomer to start a showing career at a fairly low level. The British Driving Society Show, where four rings are running all day to accommodate hundreds of exhibitors, is not suitable for a first outing. The nearest County or Agricultural Show is probably equally unsuitable. Blaring loud speakers, large crowds, parades of livestock, hot-air balloons, helicopter rides and marching bands are likely to frighten a novice animal. Horses may be silly at times but they do have incredibly good memories and unfortunately never seem to forget an unhappy experience. So, it is very important to choose the right occasion for this introduction into the horse's and Whip's career of showing in private driving classes.

It is not necessarily a good idea to choose a local, small show just because it is nearby and has along with the show-jumping, ponies, gymkhana and hunters, an open private driving class. Such an occasion may be run by someone who has little experience of the needs of driving competitors. Harness exhibitors require more space for unboxing than those entering other classes and to some extent it is more important than for ridden exhibits for their ring to have a flat surface. Also, for safety, the arena has to be larger than is often realised. The ideal show at which to start is one which is being organised specially for carriage drivers by a Driving Society official or established driving club. The needs of the driving competitors will be known and are likely to be provided. Such a show will probably have a large variety of classes. There may be a class for novice horses, or novice drivers, or both. There might be one for exercise carts in which those with pneumatic tyres are acceptable. Classes for harness horses in hand may be included as might those for harness horses which are ridden.

58 *Lara Mockridge driving Romany Lee to a Bennington Buggy, accompanied by the judge, Mr Les McCall, on her way to winning the Junior Whip Championship at the British Driving Society Show in 1990.*

59 *Winners of the Concours d'Elegance at the Horse of the Year Show in London. Monnington Granados, a Morgan stallion, driven to an American Dog Cart Phaeton by Valerie Beckum. The property of Seal-master Draught and Weather Seals.*

These are judged in the same way as a riding-horse class. The open driving classes will probably be divided by height. There may be a separate class for animals of hackney type. Such horses or ponies do not have to be pure registered hackneys. This class is for horses or ponies which have hackney type action and have hackney type conformation. Junior Whips will probably have a class which is judged entirely on their driving capabilities. Disabled drivers may also have a class of their own. There could be classes for pairs, tandems and other multiples. There may be a road drive organised. This is not a race and is not driven against the clock. It is purely for the pleasure of driving in an area, such as a park, near the show ground. If the drive is included as part of one of the showing classes, it is usual for the judge to be taken in a car, by a steward, so that he can stop at intervals along the route to see how horses are behaving. Those which pull hard, or misbehave in any other way, will be noted. Sometimes a Concours d'Elegance is included which is usually judged by an artist who chooses the turn-out which he would most like to paint. The schedule has to be read carefully and the entries sent off before the closing date. There is nothing more maddening for show secretaries, who are almost always working in an honorary capacity, to have their evening meal interrupted repeatedly by people telephoning with late entries.

Once the entry is made, preparation for the show day needs careful planning. There is a lot to be done. Horse, harness, vehicle, lamps, whip, driver's and groom's dress and travelling arrangements have all to be organised so that nothing is left to chance. It is essential to have a full dress rehearsal a few days before the show to make certain that everything fits. Quite often, new pieces may have been added to the show harness during the winter. It can be found that a collar which fitted in the autumn is too large or small the following spring. If a new collar has been made, it will need to be worn on several occasions before the show to enable it to settle into shape and not make the horse sore. Work may have been done on the vehicle, or new lamps bought and if everything is not tried before arriving at a show there is almost always something which does not fit. Also, from the Whip's point of view, the angle of the driving seat on the show vehicle is bound to feel different from the exercising vehicle. It is essential to have some practice in case the seat or foot rest is not comfortable. The horse, too, will find the vehicle different and needs to be given time to get used to how it pulls. It is not sensible to make the show ring the place for his debut in the show carriage or his new collar.

The conditioning and preparation of the horse, for showing, will probably take place over several months leading up to the show season. Building of desired muscles with correct and careful work can take years. Feeding and fittening in general has to follow a carefully planned programme. The addition of feed supplements will ensure that the animal's coat is gleaming. Cooked linseed is useful for this. Assuming that the horse is in show condition, as far as his shape and coat are concerned, it is the week or so leading up to the show which needs a lot of thought. There is so much more to getting a driving turn-out ready for a show than a riding or in-hand animal. The horse may need his jaw line, heels, mane and tail trimmed or pulled if he is of a type to which this is done. Broadly speaking, if his heels are trimmed it is correct to plait the mane. If his heels are left untrimmed, as with a Welsh Section A pony or a Welsh Cob, which is shown in hand, then the mane and tail are left loose. Some harness cobs look well with their manes hogged and this is quite acceptable. Such an animal would, of course, have his tail banged and his heels trimmed right out. All trimming needs to be completed about four days before the show, to give any clipper or scissor marks time to mellow. Feeding, as the show day is nearing, must be carefully considered. It is usually unwise to increase such feed as oats, in the last forty-eight hours, as these may go to the animal's head and make him stupid. Better by far for this first show to have him too quiet rather than the opposite. It is probably safer to feed in the normal way.

If the exhibitor is someone who has no help with the preparation for a show, it is best to spread the work over four days. The horse-box or truck should be filled with fuel. Oil, water and battery levels should be topped up. Tyre pressures, including the spares, should be checked as should the lights. Trailer indicators and brake lights should be tested with the side lights both off and on. The horse will, perhaps, need to be newly shod. This is best done about four days before the show in order to give the shoes time to seat into the feet. The vehicle can be cleaned and prepared for loading, on the third day. The show harness can be cleaned on the second day.

The day before the show needs to be reserved for the loading up of vehicle, hitching up of trailer, thorough exercising and cleaning of the horse and general preparation of everything for the journey. Clothes, picnics, hay-nets, water carriers, horse feed and rugs for wet, cold, hot or sweaty conditions must all be got ready. Travelling boots, bandages, knee pads and tail guard must be looked out. A list of items is essential if nothing is to be forgotten. By the time the morning of the show finally arrives, there should not be too much to do. Plenty of time must be left for the few jobs and the journey. There is nothing more worrying for a horse than an agitated handler who is in a hurry. A little Pax does not go amiss at this time. The horse should be given his break-fast and left in peace to finish it whilst his owners eat theirs. He can then be plaited, groomed and dressed ready for travelling. The journey should be steady and smooth so that he travels without getting upset. The system which is practised at the show, on arrival, will relate to knowledge gained from taking him to rallies. If he needed long reining or lungeing at a rally, then he is even more likely to need it at a show. If he is quite unperturbed by the whole thing, then he can be harnessed and put to when the time nears for his class. Past experience from attending rallies will give the handler the knowledge of how much, if any, work his horse needs to produce him at his best. Some horses need an hour before they settle. Others can be unboxed, walked about to relieve any stiffness and taken straight into the ring. No two are alike.

It is as well to arrive in plenty of time to be able to unload the vehicle in a leisurely manner. It will need cleaning after being transported, brass will have to be given a final polish, lamps and whip put into their holders and cushions may need to be brushed again. The number will have to be fixed to the back of the vehicle. At a small show, it will probably have to be collected from the secretary's tent on arrival. This job can be delegated to someone who is anxious to help but is really in the way. The horse will need tidying up after travelling. Harness has to be put on quietly. The driver will probably be dressed and covered with an overall to keep off any dirt whilst harnessing and putting to. The horse is put to and a final check is made of the harness etc. The driver puts on hat, gloves and apron and mounts.

The horse can be walked about until the time comes to go into the ring. In the collecting ring, it is wise to avoid any fiery or difficult look-ing horses who may upset your newcomer. It is best to try to follow someone who appears calm, with a quiet horse. The class will be called into the ring. The secret is to allow plenty of space between turn-outs. There is room, then, to pull up or to drive out of trouble if anyone has a problem. Novice drivers tend to get into a bunch in one part of the arena. Some then become hidden from the judge. The experienced Whip will be seen always to have a space in front into which to send the horse when the moment comes to show him to full advantage to the judge. The class will probably go into the ring in a clockwise direction as directed by the judge's steward. The judge will stand in the middle and note each turn-out as it drives past. Some judges keep turn-outs walking for a while whilst others prefer to see them trotting immedi-ately. The question which is always asked is: at what is the driving judge looking? The answer is simple: everything.

The first impression is very important. The judge will probably be looking for a well-proportioned turn-out in which the horse is of a suitable type for the vehicle to which he is being driven. The outline of both the horse and the Whip will be noted. Colours should be comple-mentary. A pink hat, green jacket, red knee rug and yellow wheels are not likely to be pleasing to the eye. The horse should be going forward, covering the ground with little apparent effort. He should not be pulling hard and tearing around as though he is in a trotting race. Quiet elegance with the correct outline and paces produces the best picture. After a few circuits of the ring, the steward may ask competitors to 'change the rein'; that is, to turn across the centre and drive off in the opposite direction. This shows whether or not animals will work correctly on both reins. It is essential with pairs or teams so that both sides are seen. Different judges have different ways of doing things. Some prefer to bring all the turn-outs into the centre of the ring, in any order, whilst others bring them in, in the order of preference, or even the reverse order of preference. Each turn-out is then inspected in detail. The horse will be examined for lumps and bumps. The odd scar is of little detriment but broken knees are not favoured. Once an animal has gone down, he may go down again. Feet are picked up and shape, condition and shoeing are noted. There is no truer saying than 'no foot, no horse' when it comes to a harness horse. The general turn-out of the horse is examined. The harness is checked for fit, cleanliness, condition and correctness of type for the horse and carriage concerned. The vehicle is scrutinised for fit, soundness, paint finish and appointments such as the lamps. These should have had their candles lit and blown out. The reason is that it is much easier to re-light a candle which has already been lit previously. A box of matches can be carried in the right-hand lamp. Now, with modern traffic conditions, no one is likely to drive on the roads by candle light. They would almost certainly get hit, before being seen, by fast moving traffic. However, the tradition remains and lamps should be carried for private driving classes.

Spares will probably be asked for and inspected. It is important to have these neatly displayed. A poor impression is made if the judge has to fumble under the seat to produce a carrier bag, from the local supermarket, which contains a few straps covered in mould with green, tarnished, buckles. The Whip's dress and apron or rug will be noted as well as the way in which he or she is sitting on the box and handling the reins and whip. If a social passenger is carried, it is correct for him or her to remain on the seat beside the Whip. If a groom is taken, instead of a social passenger, his or her job is to stand at the horse's head, in order to assist if the need arises. They should accompany the turn-out, when it is moving, so that they are available if there is a problem. The clothes which are worn by grooms, whether male or female, should be neat, tidy and practical. Girls' hair looks best if it is secured in a hairnet; men's hair should be neat and not hanging over the shoulders. Some girls wear riding hats and others prefer felt hats; male grooms are correct in a bowler. Tailored jackets and riding trousers or slacks, for ladies, can look smart as do suits for men. Gloves should be worn. Polished boots or shoes look well. If the occasion is dressy then livery can be worn with top hat, livery coat, breeches and boots. A stock with a plain pin to keep it in place is used. It is important for the groom, whether male or female, to appear as a smart and upright figure. A round-backed, overweight, long-haired, groom can ruin the overall impression of an otherwise excellent turn-out.

Once the turn-out has been inspected, each will probably be told to give an individual show. The Whip will ask the horse to walk forward out of line. Any tendency to nappiness or collar shyness will be noted. The walk should show a free moving, regular, four time beat. Some horses refuse to walk but jog in a two-time pace. This will not help their placing when the final choice is made. It is then usual to trot in a straight line away from the judge and, maintaining the same rhythm, turn and trot back when the straightness of the action will be noted. The turn-out will stop by the judge, halt, rein back a few steps and then walk forward and halt. The Whip should salute the judge before returning to his place in the line.

Saluting is easier for ladies than for gentlemen. A lady has to keep her reins in her left hand whilst the right hand is raised to put the whip in an horizontal position. She should turn her head slightly and give a small bow. A smile does not go amiss. Gentlemen Whips have to raise their hat with their right hand when they salute. So, the whip, as well as the reins, has to be held in the left hand. It is secured, under the thumb, over the top of the reins. When the time comes to drive at a big show, the salute to the Royal Box is given, in this way, on the first occasion of passing it on entering the ring, and on the last occasion before leaving the arena. Lady passengers should give a slight bow, male passengers should raise their hats. If a groom, in livery, is carried, he should neither turn his head, nor remove his hat. If, however, the occasion is very formal, then the male grooms should remove their hats and place them on their knees. They should also do this if the Coachman is addressed by Royalty. When waiting in line, whilst other competitors are giving their shows, it is important to keep the horse standing up as smartly as possible. If the weather is cold, it is permissible to throw a rug over the horse's loins to keep him from getting chilled. This quarter sheet can be kept in the boot of the vehicle.

When the judge has seen each competitor individually he will probably send everyone out for a few final circuits before bringing them back in order of preference. Prizes and rosettes are then presented. The judge's decision must be accepted, with a smile. *Never ever* argue. However disappointing the result and however much it seems as if the judge needs his or her eyes testing, refrain from showing disapproval; the judge's decision is always final. It is irreversable and getting cross does no good, but only a great deal of harm to the exhibitor concerned. Few people, other than the immediate connections, will agree with a disgruntled competitor. A reputation for being a bad loser will stay for life. No one ever forgets this display of bad manners. It must be remembered that the result is purely the opinion of one person. There is probably another show next week, with a different judge who could reverse the order. Judges place animals on how they go on the day and this can so easily vary from show to show, which is what makes it all such fun. Fortunately, different judges like different kinds of turn-outs. If they did not have varying opinions, there would not be much point in exhibiting. The horse can be taken to bigger shows as experience and confidence are gained. It will probably not be long before he will accept all the sights and sounds at a big show which would have caused terror and problems on his first outing.

Driving trials

Some people like to be competitive but do not like the result of a competition to rest entirely on the opinion of one person, as it does in the judging of a showing class. They prefer to try to win on their performance. Horse Driving Trials are judged mainly on this criterion. A driving event is usually divided into three sections and is similar, in many ways, to a ridden event. Competition A consists of Dressage. Competition B is the Marathon and Competition C is the Cone Driving. The three sections correspond to the dressage, cross country and show-jumping stages of a ridden event.

Numerous driving trials are organised at both club and national level, throughout the season, with classes ranging from pre-novice for complete newcomers with single turn-outs, to those for international four-in-hand drivers. Before competing in an event, it is wise to go to a horse driving trial as a spectator to see what it is all about. Careful study of the programme at a national event, which is likely to include maps of the cross-country and cones courses and diagrams of the obstacles (sometimes called hazards), will be very informative. Much can be learnt by seeing how competitors drive the various obstacles and why they take certain routes to get the fastest times. The rules for these competitions are based on regulations laid down by the F.E.I., the International Equestrian Federation, in Switzerland. Copies of national rules, which are based on these international regulations, are obtainable from The British Horse Driving Trials Association and from driving societies throughout the world. Time should be taken to read these in order to understand how trials are run.

A section called Presentation is sometimes included for novices at club level. It is judged at the halt before the dressage test is driven. The purpose of this is to keep the standard of turnout high and to prevent accidents due to the danger of ill fitting or worn harness or an unsound vehicle. Marks are given for the driver and groom which covers their dress, the driver's position on the box, handling of reins and whip and the groom's handling of the horse if the need arises. Marks for the vehicle include fit, balance, cleanliness, appointments and spares kit. The marks for the horse are for condition, turnout, shoeing and general cleanliness. Marks are awarded for the fit of the harness,

60 *The author, accompanied by Mrs Frank Hales, driving Razali to a Harewood Sporting Gig, in the dressage phase at the Brighton Driving Trials in 1983 when they won the single pony class and qualified for the National Championships at Windsor. The one-handed thirty metre circle is being executed at collected trot.*

condition and cleaniness. There is a final mark for the overall impression.

Judges are not, in this case, trying to find a winner. It is as possible to get a row of tens with a set of carefully maintained and cleaned exercise harness and a shining general purpose vehicle as it is for someone to get low marks for a dirty set of patent-trimmed harness and an ill-fitting show carriage pulled by an overweight horse, handled by a scruffy groom. Some events have an optional competition for presentation which is judged separately, for those who want to try to win this section. It is popular with some grooms who take a great pride in the turnout of their charges.

At advanced levels of competition, presentation is judged whilst the dressage test is being driven with a mark being given for the overall impression. Standards have risen so dramatically during the past few years that these experienced competitors often get eight (good), nine (very good), or even ten (excellent) out of ten on their mark sheets. It has to be remembered that ten for excellent does not mean ten for perfect. So, it is possible for the judges to give a ten without close scrutiny. At national levels of competition there are three judges sitting around the dressage arena at B, C and E and their marks are averaged.

The Dressage Test fills some competitors with far greater fear than the Marathon course. It should not cause this worry because it is, after all, purely the correct basic training of the horse upon which his whole performance rests. The purpose of the test is to show the judge, or judges, that the horse is calm and obedient to carry out the wishes of his driver. Impulsion, regularity of paces, lightness and correct outline will be judged as will control and accuracy of the test.

It is important to prepare, well in advance, for the day when the test has to be driven. As the test must be driven from memory, it is essential to learn the sequence so that concentration can be directed on how the horse is going rather than frantically trying to remember which movement comes next. A copy of the test must be obtained from the event organiser. The easiest way to learn the test is to get a piece of paper and draw the same number of rectangles as there are movements. The arena measurements of eighty metres by forty metres, for a single turnout, is easy to put onto paper to scale. First of all, it is essential to become familiar with the arena letters. One easy way to remember them is, starting at A at the bottom centre and going round in an anti-clockwise direction: A Fat Black Manx Cat Had Eight Kittens. The letters R S V P are easier to remember once you can relate to where R is placed. P, B and R are similarly shaped which is a help. X is in the middle. D lies between F and K and is where you sometimes go Down the centre line. G lies between M and H. G is where the final salute is given before Going out of the arena at the end of the test. The letters I and L are sometimes used and I can be remembered by Royal International Show as it lies between R and S. The letter L is between P and V.

As each movement is read, it can be drawn onto one of the rectangles and a pattern will form some kind of logic and make more sense.

It is wise to set up an arena at home so that the horse can get used to working in an arena of the correct shape and size. Failure to do this will result in a bad test because the arena can seem to be very small. The positions of D L X I and G should be marked with sawdust, white paint or creosote. Plenty of time needs to be given to practising driving straight down the centre line from A to C over the top of these marked places. It is also wise to put white planks at the corners and alongside the side letters so that the horse gets used to seeing these. The side letters should be put in their correct places. It is a good idea to park a 'judge's car at C to familiarise the horse with the sight of this before his first outing at a competition.

It is a good plan to walk the test in the arena until it is thoroughly learnt. For some reason, it is also necessary to alter the letters and be able to walk it from either end. It is possible to get into a state of mind which is confusing if the arena at the event, for some illogical reason, seems to have been put 'the wrong way round' in the Whip's mind. Nerves can play havoc at times like this. It is very often due to the presence of trees or hedges which remind one subconsciously of similar trees or hedges at home. The horse should not be made to drive the actual test too many times. He will learn it far too well, and anticipate the movements, which will cause difficulties and remarks on the dressage sheet such as 'anticipation of movement', as he smartly reins back before the ten-second halt is over.

One of the most common faults with beginners is failing to use the whole arena. It must be remembered that the arena is there to be used. Think of each corner as a quarter circle and go straight wherever possible, keeping to the sides. For example, do not cut from G to M when what is meant is from G, down to C and then a quarter circle right, towards the corner, and a quarter circle right towards M. Inaccurate, or jerky transitions are another failing. The transition from trot to walk at say C, means that the horse should be brought smoothly down to walk so that he walks when his nose gets level with C, and progresses forward, and does not come to a half halt and then walk forward. Transitions from walk to trot are the same. The horse should move quietly and smoothly into trot when his nose is level with the letter and not jump forward with a jerk.

Inaccuracy of figures is often seen. Circles have to be round. A very common fault is for the first half of a circle to be round and the second

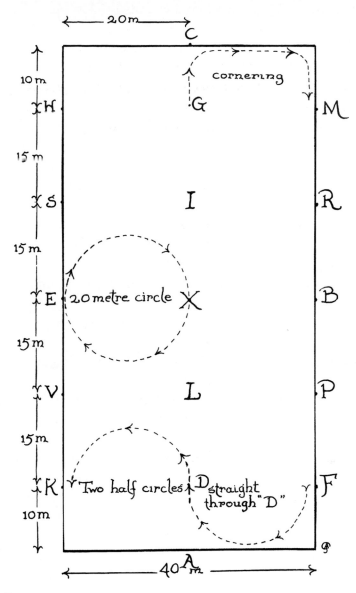

Fig. 18 *Dressage arena*

half flat as the driver heads back too quickly to the marker. A circle of twenty metres, B X B, means that the circle should begin at B and that the horse should pass over X so that the shafts and wheels lie either side of X and then return to B to complete the circle. Another common inaccuracy of figure is when two half circles have to be driven such as K D twenty-metre half circle right, D F twenty-metre half circle left. It is important to go straight, momentarily, through D. Many people drive diagonally over the centre mark. Common faults, with circles, and half circles, are caused by animals which fall in. In an effort to hold them out, the head and neck becomes bent away from the direction of the circle and the remark is then 'wrong bend' or 'looking out'. This is caused by the horse being held out by the outside rein.

Some tests, at novice level, ask for a few strides of lengthened trot. The lengthened strides are usually shown across the diagonal, through X. The most common fault, in this movement, is that the horse is made to hurry and runs rather than lengthens. The hoof beats should remain at the same tempo and the hind feet should overtrack the marks which the front feet are making as the horse stretches his stride to cover more ground. In working trot, the hind feet should go exactly into the marks which the front feet are making.

Failure to halt squarely and for the full time of perhaps ten seconds is a common fault. Many horses step back just after they have halted, probably because the vehicle first tightens the breeching and then rolls back a little, so the horse steps back to take the weight off his collar.

Resistance to the rein back is often seen when the horse braces himself, hollows his back and refuses to step backwards. The rein back should be straight. The secret here is to be certain that the reins are absolutely level before the animal is asked to rein back. An even feel must be kept on both reins. The movement should be in diagonal two time. Plenty of home work may be needed to be certain of this.

There is no reason why an average animal should not be trained at home, by his owner, to perform an accurate and obedient dressage test. The horse does not have to be an exceptional mover although, of course, it is a great help if he does have natural ability to move well. The main thing to remember is that he must be correctly and carefully educated so that he fully understands what is required. A row of reasonable marks can be obtained if enough work is put in during the preceding months. If the driver can ride this is a great help as the work to produce a good driven test is exactly the same as with ridden dressage. There is, of course, no canter or lateral work. It is, in many ways, more difficult in harness as there is no seat or legs to give the aids. Everything has to come from the hands, the whip and the voice, which is allowed in driven dressage. The horse will eventually learn what is wanted and will perform a good test without the help of legs and seat.

Work on the long reins, as described in *Breaking a Horse to Harness*, can produce very good results. The author works her ponies under saddle and on the circle, on long reins, as much, if not more, than she does in a vehicle to obtain the desired obedience, impulsion, paces and outline for a good test.

The purpose of the Marathon, known as Competition B, is to test the fitness and stamina of the horse or pony. It is the equivalent of the cross-country phase of a ridden event. It is a great test of horsemanship as correct judgement of pace is essential. Instead of cross-country fences, there are obstacles, in Section E, which have to be negotiated against the clock. Artificial obstacles are constructed where no natural hazards can be used or to augment the existing natural hazards. Each is numbered and lettered. The routes through these hazards are also a considerable test of intelligence and memory. Time spent in reconnaissance is never wasted. The obstacles need to be walked, several times, on foot and the chosen routes thoroughly learnt. Failure to do this will make it almost impossible to drive each obstacle correctly, in the shortest possible time.

The Marathon can be divided into five sections, namely; A, B, C, D, and E of varying speeds and paces. At Club level, there may be just one, two or perhaps three sections. A horse needs to be very fit, if he is to complete the Marathon phase without strain or distress. It is extremely demanding and a careful fitness programme must be planned. The type of fitness required must not be underestimated; it is similar to that needed for winning a high-class hunter trial. In order to have an animal ready to compete in a three-day event in May, the horse needs to be worked, seriously, every day from the end of January. Work will start with walking exercise and gradually be built up over the weeks and months. Feeding must depend on work and will be increased as peak fitness is reached. Every animal has to be worked and fed as an individual as no two are alike.

Training for obstacles can be carried out without much problem. If there is woodland available, it is a good plan to clear areas between trees where schooling can take place. The horse can be taught to weave in and out of tight places without becoming frightened. It is a good idea to put the horse in an open bridle and with saddle and crupper take him on long reins to the tree hazards. He can see where he is being asked to go and will twist and turn happily in and out of the trees without worry.

61 *Heather Kinner and Language Timothy successfully negotiating an obstacle at the Normanhurst Horse Driving Trials in 2001 when they won the single pony class.*

When he is confident, he can be long reined in a blinkered bridle. He can then be put to and driven in the cross-country vehicle. It is best not to ask, too soon, for tight turns when the vehicle may get jammed against a tree trunk and he could get frightened. If, during a schooling session, the vehicle does get jammed, it is probably wiser to dismount quietly, take him out of the vehicle and lead him out of the trees than to frighten him by forcing him to disentangle the vehicle. Some horses, understandably, become very worried when the vehicle gets jammed solidly. They just cannot think why, all of a sudden, their pulling is ineffective. It is simpler to take him out of the shafts and put him back in again, away from the trees and have another try. The experience gained will be invaluable to the driver in that it will make him realise that his angle of approach to the gap was wrong.

It is a good plan to set up one or two measured kilometre distances so that some idea of the timing of pace is achieved. A stop-watch can be carried by the passenger or put on the dashboard so that it can be seen exactly how fast a kilometre needs to be driven in order not to get time faults. It will be found that the walk section, in particular, can be difficult to achieve with some shorter striding animals and make the trainer aware of the work needed to lengthen the animal's stride.

Time must be spent on training the horse to cross water without hesitation. Some horses have an inbuilt fear of water and it can take many months of patience in order to build confidence. Early training can begin with making the horse go through every available puddle. Once confidence is gained with these, then the search begins for small, hard bottomed, water crossings. It is worth taking the trouble to travel the animal, in a horse-box, in order to train with the right kind of water crossing. The ideal training ground is a shallow, gently flowing river which has a stony approach and exit. The horse can be led or long reined in an open bridle behind another horse as school master, to gain confidence. He can then be long reined in blinkers and finally put to

62 *Trina Hall driving a clear round with Samuel Pepys at an event.*

137

and driven. It is important to go to several different water crossings so that he will eventually face whatever water he meets at an event. On no account must he ever be taken into a soft-bottomed, muddy water crossing as this will, understandably, frighten him and make him suspicious. It will do harm rather than good.

It is safer for the passenger to be carried on the rear of the vehicle than on the seat alongside the driver, for all cross-country schooling and competing. Hard hats should be worn by both.

The purpose of the cones course, known as Competition C, is to test the obedience, suppleness and fitness of the animal, after the marathon. It is also designed to test the skill of the competitor. The cones course is the equivalent to the show-jumping phase of a ridden event. It is quite possible for a competitor, who was winning after the dressage and marathon phases, to go down several placings after Competition C, if he does not drive a clear round within the time allowed.

The course is erected using cones which have balls on their tops. If the ball falls from the cone, then the obstacle is deemed to have been hit. Faults are then incurred. Faults are also given for exceeding the time allowed and for disobediences which are similar to those in show jumping, such as circling, stopping or reining back before an obstacle. Enthusiastic grooms and/or passengers must be given strict instructions *not* to indicate the direction to the driver as such assistance results in elimination.

Schooling for the Cones section is as important as for the other two phases. Cones can be purchased and it is worth buying a few. Failure to practise this section can lose a competition very easily. The cones can be put quite wide apart, to begin with. The horse can again be taken through, on long reins, in an open bridle. The main thing to teach him is that whenever he is faced with a pair of cones, and from whatever angle, he must go right through the centre. Work in blinkers follows and then he can be put to the vehicle and driven. The secret of a clear round is to line the horse's ears up with the centre of the gap between the cones and go forward in a positive manner. Such confidence usually results in clear rounds. Hesitant approaches, with hands which are moving all over the place, can cause a competition to be lost by the toppling of one little ball.

When the time comes to compete at a trial, most of what has been said about preparing for a show applies to getting ready for an event. It is important to arrive early so that there is plenty of time for studying maps and for walking the cross-country obstacles and the Cones course. Calculations will have to be made regarding the timing of each kilometre on a section. A lot of competitors put such vital information as the kilometre timings and the routes through the obstacles on a sheet of paper which they tape to a panel on the vehicle where it can easily be read, along the route, by the driver and the groom. The stop-watch can also be fixed in a similar position.

Events are run strictly to time, in order to get all the competitors through the course, so it is essential to take careful note of the starting time, on the time sheet, and be a little ahead of the stated time for each section. The main thing to remember about competing in a driving trial is that it is taking part and completing the course, without distress to the horse, which matters. Being well placed is a bonus.

Pair driving

63 *The author driving her full brother Connemara ponies, Scottsway Sunrise and Scottsway Sunset to a Fenix Spider Phaeton.*

By the time that the driver has reached the stage of attending rallies and competing successfully at shows or events, with a single turn-out, thoughts often turn to the possibility of a pair. Whichever type of animal has proved satisfactory hitherto will probably be favoured and the search is likely to begin for a match to the one already owned. People who have a particular breed of horse are at an advantage because the breeds often produce animals which are true to type. Research into blood lines and visits to studs could result in a match being found. It will not be easy – but then nothing ever is when it comes to finding a suitable animal, let alone a match for an existing one.

The ideal pair should be of the same type. If one is heavy and one light they can never be called a real pair. Their quarters should match for breadth and their heads should be of the same width. They should be the same length and same height. They should match for colour and have the same markings. Their stride needs to be the same so that their action will match. In fact, in the words of the late Sanders Watney, 'A perfect pair should look like one horse twice.'

Pair driving has similar handling of the reins to that used with a single horse. There are only two reins and these are held in the same way which makes the progression not too difficult as far as the rein handling is concerned.

Pairs are usually driven to four-wheeled vehicles. They are occasionally driven to a two-wheeler such as with a Curricle, when a Curricle bar is used with the harness. The Cape Cart is another pair horse, two-wheeler, when Cape harness is used, but this is comparatively rare. In Holland, Friesian horses are put, in pair, with belly bugle harness to two-wheeled Friesian Chaises. If a pair is being considered, the search

64 *A Waggonette.*

for a suitable carriage begins. Vehicles such as Phaetons and Four-Wheeled Dog Carts are ideal for showing. Specially made, modern four-wheelers are needed for eventing. Waggonettes and carriages of that type are useful for such occasions as rallies. Six people can be accommodated. The driver and one passenger are carried on the forward-facing front seat and four more people can be seated on the inward-facing rear seats, enabling friends to be taken along for the ride.

Pair harness

The bridle

The harness for a pair differs quite considerably from that used for single horses, with the exception of the bridles. Care must be taken over the types of bit to be used with a pair. Liverpool bits with movable cheek pieces are frequently used for single driving but are unsuitable for use with a pair other than with the rough cheek attachment of the reins. If the reins are put onto plain cheek it will be seen that the coupling reins cause the rings of the bits to turn and cause severe pinching on the inner sides of both horse's muzzles. This is why bits such as Buxton, Butterfly and Elbow (Army Reversible) were designed, as they have no part of their rings in front of the actual mouth piece of the bit. Therefore, when the coupling reins are buckled to the rings, or further down the cheek, the side of the bit is able to turn and there is no part which presses on the side of the muzzle. Liverpool bits with fixed cheeks are suitable for use with a pair because the cheeks do not turn wherever the reins are buckled. Bits with bars across the bottom are often used to prevent the reins from becoming caught in the cheeks of the bits. The noseband, for a pair, should be put onto the cheek

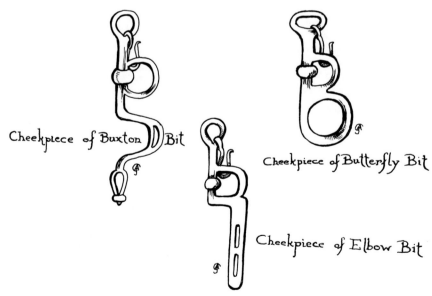

Cheekpiece of Buxton Bit

Cheekpiece of Butterfly Bit

Cheekpiece of Elbow Bit

Fig. 19 *Types of bit*

143

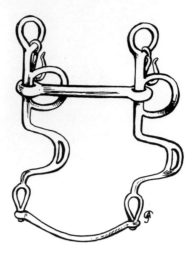

Fig. 20 *Buxton bit*

pieces so that it buckles on the outer side. The nearside horse's bridle has the noseband fastening from the nearside and the offside horse's bridle has the noseband fastening from the offside.

The breast collar

The breast part of the collar will be found to be longer than one which is made for single harness because the tug buckles are fastened, by means of small straps, to the pad. These tug buckles are of a different design from those used with single harness. There is a dee, at the top, onto which is fixed a small

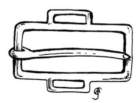

Fig. 21 *Pair tug buckle*

strap and buckle which, in turn, is fastened to a point sewn to a dee below the terrets on the pad. There is another dee at the bottom of the tug buckle, which has a point of leather to take the false belly band. It is for these reasons that a single breast collar is not suitable for use with a pair. The traces are put onto the tug buckles. With traditional leather harness, care should be taken that the traces are put onto the correct side so that quick release ends or release points at the vehicle end are facing outwards, enabling them to be reached from the outer sides of each horse. The false martingale is buckled to the centre dee, at the front of the collar. The dee which is attached to the side of the centre of the breast part of the collar is to take the pole strap.

144

The collar and hames

The same collar can be worn for pair driving as for single. The hames which are used on the collar for a pair differ from those employed with a single. They have a kidney link and kidney link ring at the bottom instead of a hame strap or hame chain and they are fastened to the collars, at the top, by hame straps as with a single turn-out. The difference is that the offside animal's hames fasten with the hame strap tightening from the offside so that the point is inwards. The nearside horse's hames are tightened onto the collar from the nearside, as with a single turn-out. The false martingale is buckled right round the collar, passing through the kidney link, at the bottom of the hames. This helps to keep the hames on the collar when pressure is put, from the pole strap, onto the kidney link ring. The hame tug, which goes from the hames to the trace buckle, is longer than that used with single harness because the trace buckle, as with breast collar pair harness, is fastened by a strap to a dee on the pad and by a point to the belly band. It is for this reason that pair hames are not suitable for use with single harness.

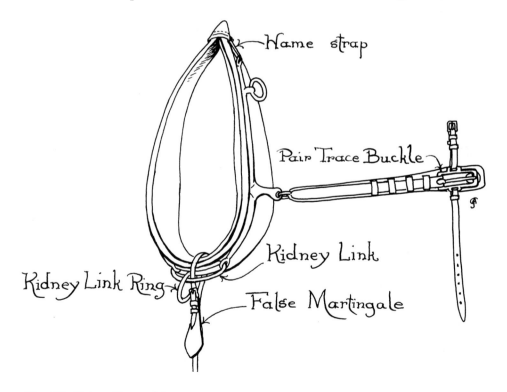

Fig. 22 *Pair collar and hames*

65 *The nearside of a set of John Willie pair harness with breast collar and breeching. The brown bridle has an elbow bit.*

Pair harness pad

This is lighter than the saddle used for single harness owing to the fact that it does not have to take any weight. It is merely an anchor point for the crupper, traces, trace carrier and breeching. If a bearing rein is used, then of course it is fixed to the bearing rein hook on the pad. The only time that heavier saddles, as opposed to pads, are used with a pair is when the vehicle is a two-wheeler, such as a Curricle, and the weight of the carriage is occasionally transmitted from the pole to the horses' backs. Traditionally made pair pads have terrets which can be unscrewed, as with single harness saddles. Modern harness made from webbing, nylon or similar materials very often has fixed dees or rings which act as terrets to take the reins. The girth and crupper are fastened as with single harness and the breeching seat is held up by a loin strap as with a single. As there are no shafts with a pair, but just a pole, the

146

breeching works in a different way. There are long points coming from each side of the breeching seat. These are buckled into both sides at the tug buckle where it joins the pad as well as into where the trace is buckled.

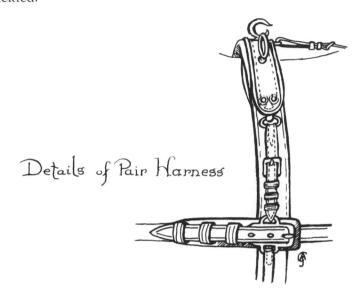

Details of Pair Harness

Fig 23 *Pair pad showing tug buckle*

Putting on pair harness

When a full collar is used it is put on first, followed by the hames in the usual way. The false martingale is fastened right round the base of the collar and passed through the kidney link. This is to help to keep the hames on the collar when strain from the pole straps, on the kidney link ring, would perhaps pull the hames from the collar. The pad, which for single harness is called a saddle, is placed on the back and the little buckles from the top dees on the hame tug buckles are fastened to holes in the point straps fixed to the small dees on the pad. This ensures that this light pad is held in place whilst the crupper is put under the tail. The girth is then passed through the martingale loop and buckled. The false belly band is also passed through the martingale loop and buckled to the point strap fixed to the lower dee on the hame tug buckle. If the traces are not already buckled to the hame tugs, these are now put on, taking care that each is the correct way round for quick release ends at the roller bolts to be reached. The traces are laid over the horse's back, with the outer trace on top of the inner trace ready for putting to.

66 *A trace on a roller bolt.*

67 *The offside of a set of pair harness with full collar and breeching. The offside trace is put on top of the nearside trace ready for putting to. The bridle has a Buxton bit.*

Breeching is not always used for pairs with full collars as the weight of pulling up is often taken by the horses through the collars, on the tops of their necks. If breeching is being used, it is either buckled into the trace tug buckles, alongside the traces, as seen in plate 65 or, as seen in plate 67 into dees at the end of the trace tug buckles. Loops, to form trace carriers, are usually fixed onto each end of the breeching seat, in a position below the loin strap. If breeching is not used, then trace carriers are sometimes employed to prevent the traces from sagging. A loin strap, which has loops fitted to each end, is passed through the back strap of the crupper. The traces are put through these loops before being fastened to the roller bolts or swingle trees.

Harnessing for a pair wearing breast collars is almost the same as with full collars. The only difference is that breeching always has to be worn – otherwise, when slowing down or going downhill, the weight of the vehicle via the pole and pole straps would push the breast collars up the

149

animals' necks. If breeching is not worn, it will be likely that the vehicle will run into the horses' quarters and hind legs, unless held by the Whip, using a brake, when he sees the pole go forward and the pole straps tighten.

The breeching points, which continue from the breeching seat, are secured in the trace buckles of the breast collars alongside the traces. This has the effect that as the pole pulls the breast collars forward so the breeching tightens and the vehicle is held back very effectively.

The reins are put on next and great care must be taken to see that they are fitted correctly. The offside horse always wears the draught rein which has the buckle at the hand end. The draught rein, which is the one with the holes punched in it and continues from the hand to the bit, always goes down the outer side of each horse. So on the offside horse the draught rein is passed through the offside pad terret and hame terret ready to be buckled to the right-hand side of the bit when the

68 *The nearside of a set of pair harness with full collar and no breeching but a trace carrier. The near-side trace is put on top of the offside trace ready for putting to.*

bridle has been put on. The coupling rein, which has a buckle where it joins the draught rein, will eventually be buckled to the right-hand side of the nearside horse's bit so that when the right rein is tightened both horses are brought to the right. This coupling rein is passed through the nearside pad terret, on the offside horse, then through his nearside hame terret and left ready to be temporarily looped through his noseband before being coupled across to the nearside horse when the pair are put to. The bridle is put on and, in the case of the offside horse, the outer, right, rein is buckled to the bit and the inner, left, rein is

Fig. 24 *Coupling rein round Liverpool bit in rough cheek position*

passed through the noseband. The point of the rein is secured by the keeper to hold the rein end in place ready for putting to and coupling to the offside of the nearside horse. Needless to say, the procedure is the same for the nearside horse's reins but is a mirror image.

If Liverpool bits with movable cheeks are being employed, the coupling reins can only be used with the reins buckled on to rough cheek position. Both draught reins can be buckled on the outer sides of each horse in the normal rough cheek position as with a single turn-out. The coupling reins are buckled onto rough cheek in a way to ensure that the front of the ring of the bit is not turned towards the muzzle. The point of the rein has to be passed right round the cheek of the bit, directly below the mouthpiece, so that the pull is entirely sideways with no twist of the ring. A lot of the unsteady heads seen on driven pairs are caused by pain created by the incorrect buckling of coupling reins onto Liverpool bits with movable mouthpieces.

Putting to a pair

69 *The pole straps on the pole-head of a four-wheeler.*

Before putting to a pair, the pole straps are fixed to the pole head with the buckles on the outer sides. Pole straps are made of strong material to enable them to take the weight of the vehicle. Pole chains are used for such team vehicles as road coaches. If pole chains are employed, care must be taken to ensure that hooks are put on in such a way that bits or bridles cannot get caught in the hooks, with obvious disastrous results. A check needs to be made that the pole pin which secures the pole to the forecarriage is fully in place and that the fifth wheel or turntable is well greased. A dried up surface on the turntable will cause the pole to jerk from side to side. The animals are led up alongside the pole from behind the carriage. Care must be taken to see that they do not catch any part of their harness on the splinter bar or roller bolts as they are brought up. First, the coupling reins are buckled. That which is lying in the noseband of the offside horse is taken across and buckled to the inner side of the nearside horse's bit and the nearside horse's coupling rein is buckled to the inner side of the offside horse's bit. The animal which has the higher head carriage has his on the top. This enables a groom to hold both horses by the coupling reins. When holding a pair, it is wise to stand a little to one side of the pole head, on the side of the most difficult animal. Tempting though it may be, grooms should never hold horses by the bars of their bits. The

70 *A pole strap through the kidney link ring on the hames on a full collar.*

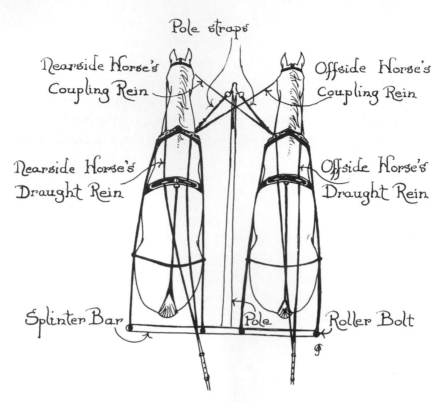

Pole straps

Nearside Horse's
Coupling Rein

Offside Horse's
Coupling Rein

Nearside Horse's
Draught Rein

Offside Horse's
Draught Rein

Splinter Bar

Pole

Roller Bolt

Fig. 25 *Pair harnessing*

severity of such handling could result in serious problems.

Next, the pole chains or pole straps are fastened loosely to the ring on the breast collar or the kidney-link ring on the hames. Competitors in driving trials prefer to take the pole straps right round the collars before passing them through the kidney-link rings, in order to be certain that the hames do not get pulled away from the collars during the cross-country competition. This is quite acceptable under such circumstances but is not correct for showing.

The traces are fastened next. The outer traces are attached first so that the horse's quarters are held alongside the pole to prevent them from swinging outwards and then pulling the pole sideways. The inner traces are fastened next. At this stage the pole straps can be taken up a few holes or the chains a few links. If they were tightened at first it would be difficult to get the traces onto the hooks or roller bolts.

The nearside rein is then thrown over both horses' backs which is why this is traditionally the one without the buckle. A buckle end flying through the air on a dark night during a quick change of horses at a Coaching Inn could have resulted in a blinded coachman as he stood by the offside horse ready to catch the rein prior to mounting.

Both reins are folded through the offside terret, on the offside horse's pad, ready for the Whip to mount. If, before mounting, the Whip or groom should notice something on the inner sides of the harness which needs altering, but cannot be reached from the outer sides, the horses must be taken from the vehicle in order to correct the error. Under no circumstances should anyone crawl between the pair to adjust harness which cannot be reached; this is highly dangerous.

In taking a pair out, the order is reversed. The nearside rein, which is on the offside as a result of dismounting on that side, is thrown over to the nearside and put up into the nearside horse's terret. The pole straps are loosened, the inner traces unfastened and the outer traces unhooked. The pole straps are undone and the coupling reins unbuckled. The horses are then led forward and carefully away, making sure that loops of harness do not get caught in the pole head.

Driving a pair and adjusting the coupling reins

The secret of pair driving lies mainly in the correct adjustment of the coupling reins. If both horses are not going straight and are unhappy in their mouths, it is unlikely that they will be able to work properly together as a pair. When putting horses into pair, even if they are ill matched for length and height, it is best to have all four traces level. Some people shorten or lengthen traces to get lazy or ill-matched horses to work as a pair. It may be a short-term answer but it is not satisfactory in the long term. Both horses should be trained and bitted correctly so that they are able to work as one in perfect unison.

Pole straps or chains should also be put on matching holes or links. They should be tight enough to ensure that the vehicle is held off the horse's quarters and hind legs in descending a hill or stopping, but not so tight that the horses' collars are being pulled inwards. The adjustment should allow some play in the pole. It is important to be sure that the pole is long enough to enable the pole straps to work properly as too short a pole will prevent this.

Should the offside horse be larger, longer and bigger altogether, he will need more room. His head will be in front of the nearside horse; his quarters will be further behind. However, his collar should be level with that of his partner, with his traces and pole straps of the same length as those of his partner. In order to understand how to adjust coupling reins, it is best to lay out a pair of pair reins on the ground and take the adjustment one step at a time. It is important to remember that, for the purpose of this explanation, the offside, right-hand, horse is much bigger and longer. He needs more length of rein to accommodate the length of his neck to allow him to work. It will be found, if the reins have been made correctly by a knowledgeable harness maker, that there are an uneven number of holes, say eleven, punched about four centimetres (an inch and a half) apart, on the draught rein.

First, fasten the coupling buckles into the centre holes, say number six, of the draught rein. Now, lay the reins on the ground with the offside rein, which is the one with the small buckle at the hand end, on the right and the nearside rein, which is the one with the point on the

71 *The author driving her pair at their first show, accompanied by Pat Zilli and Peter Durrant.*

end, on the left. It will be seen, with reins made to fit 14.2 hand animals, that the length of the coupling reins is about fifteen centimetres (six inches) longer than that of the draught reins. This is to allow for the extra distance which is needed when the coupling reins are taken across to each animal in coupling them together. This would probably be exactly how the reins would be coupled for a perfectly matched pair. If this ill-assorted pair, who for the purpose of this explanation are probably over a hand apart in height, were harnessed with the reins in this position, the shorter animal would have to do all the work. He would be on a much looser rein than his long-necked partner who would be restricted by a tight rein not long enough to allow for the length of his neck. So, in order to allow this bigger animal to do his share of the work, his reins have to be lengthened. First, the coupling buckle on the offside rein is altered to allow the draught rein to lengthen through the buckle, say five holes, which loosens the contact on the right side of his mouth by nineteen centimetres (seven and a half inches, or five holes by one and a half inches). The left side of his mouth must now be loosened by the same amount – so the coupling rein from the nearside horse must be taken forwards towards his partner's mouth, five holes. In this example, the nearside coupling buckle has been moved forward to lengthen the nearside rein to the offside horse and the offside buckle has been moved backwards to lengthen the offside rein to the offside horse. Thus, both reins to the offside horse have been lengthened.

Although this can be difficult to understand when reading the instructions, it is quite simple when the reins are put on the ground and the system is tried out stage by stage. Normally, any difference in the coupling with a pair which are reasonably well matched will be found to be one or two holes, up and down the draught reins from the centre hole, to give four centimetres (one and a half inches) or seven and a half centimetres (three inches) of extra rein to one or other horse. The main thing to remember is that, providing the reins were made properly in the first place, coupling buckles should be placed in the central hole at the beginning. If one is lengthened in one direction then the opposite must be shortened the same number of holes in the opposite direction for horses which do not match. If both horses are going with their heads turned inwards it probably means that both coupling reins are too short and both need letting out the same number of holes in the same direction. Equally, if both horses have their heads turned outwards, the coupling reins may need to be shortened as both are too long.

Once coupling reins have been adjusted so that the horses are working together, great care has to be taken that they are always buckled into their correct holes. It is best to write the hole numbering onto a piece of paper to be kept on the vehicle or in the harness room, for easy reference. This is another reason for always putting the buckled-ended rein on the offside horse.

The two most common mistakes made with harnessing and putting to a pair are that the coupling reins either get forgotten or each is buckled to the same horse as its draught rein. This gives some brakes but no steering at all. The other most common fault is for the draught and coupling reins to be put on the wrong sides when harnessing so that one or both horses will go with their heads turned inwards. If, on setting off, one head appears to be bent one way or another, check that the coupling and draught parts of the rein have been put and buckled onto the correct sides.

Another fault is for the offside and nearside reins to be put on the wrong animals which, if they are an unmatched pair, causes headaches until the mistake is noticed by someone, by looking at the hand end for the little buckle. Of course, if the horses are perfectly matched, the problems of coupling will not exist as they will almost certainly be buckled on the central holes and will go straight at all times.

It is a good plan regularly to change the sides on which the horses are put, so that each will work equally well on either side of the pole. This helps to prevent the bad habit of pulling away from or leaning against the pole from developing. Once horses learn to do this, there is very little that can be done to stop this disagreeable habit. Horses can get so bad that they eventually become almost undrivable.

The pair should work so that they are absolutely straight with equal tension on all four traces. It is often found that one of a pair does more work than the other, in spite of the coupling reins being correctly adjusted. Some animals become very skilled at keeping their traces just tight enough to give the appearance that they are working when, in fact, their partner is actually doing all the work. It is important to work each animal, as a single, so that correct basic training is established to produce good paces and outline. Providing that the horses have worked correctly as singles, they will be likely to go in exactly the same way when they are put to as a pair and there should not be too many problems.

The handling of the reins and whip is similar to a single but it will be found that the reins go away from the hands with a wider pull. To begin with, this gives the feeling of sideways stretch to the fingers. There is, of course, more weight in the hands if the animals start to pull. The feeling when turning is 'deader' than with a single. This is because part of the contact is being taken by the coupling reins with a sideways contact on the mouth instead of direct contact as with a single. Also, as the inner horse comes round, he pulls the pole head with his collar, through the pole straps. This brings the forecarriage of the vehicle round. So, the whole turn has a more sideways pull than has a single between shafts. It will also be found, during a tight turn, that the horses come round at a right angle to the box which affects the contact between the driver and his horses.

It has to be realised that, when cornering, the outer animal has to lengthen his stride and the inner animal has to shorten his stride in order to maintain smoothness through the turn. It is important to steady and balance the pair before cornering. There is great satisfaction when the pair go so well together that they work as one horse twice, trotting stride for stride, in regular two time.

159

Tandem driving

There is no reason why the same two animals should not go equally well in both pair and tandem. Providing that their basic training has been correct, they will be capable of being driven as a pair on one day and as a tandem the next day, with no difficulty. From the moment during putting to that they are brought up alongside the pole, or placed one in front of the other, they will know what is wanted and there will not be any problems. The advantages of progressing to a tandem instead of a pair are that less equipment needs to be purchased and the horses do not have to match in the same way as they do with a pair. They look smarter if they are of the same colour and type but it is quite usual to have a leader which is a more spectacular mover with greater quality than the wheeler, who can be of more solid build to do all the work. A lot of fun can be had with an unmatched tandem, though the result may not be as successful when it comes to showing.

The two-wheeled vehicle which has been used for single driving can be employed with a tandem. It is easier to drive a tandem to a two-wheeler than a four-wheeled carriage because the articulation of this adds to the problems, if the horses should also decide to articulate. If something causes the leader to turn to face his driver and go in the opposite direction from the vehicle and the wheeler follows, the forecarriage will turn at an angle from the body of the vehicle. The resulting muddle can be imagined and could be difficult to disentangle. If a two-wheeler is used and both horses decide to turn quickly and go back in the direction from where they have just come, the vehicle will turn with the wheeler and there is less of a problem to sort out.

A lot of the harness, for the wheeler, is also the same as with a single.

The art of tandem driving was summed up, in the late nineteenth century, by a horse dealer who is reputed to have said, 'I always look upon a man as drives a tandem as a fool; he makes two hosses do the work of one and most likely breaks his silly neck.' This may be true, but for anyone who wishes to progress from single and pair and is searching for thrills and excitement, then tandem driving is the answer. It requires light, sensitive hands and an alert brain to produce a straight, free moving tandem. Things can go wrong with lightning speed but there is little to compare with the wonderful feeling of sitting up behind an onward-going, light-mouthed and obedient tandem.

In many ways, tandem is more difficult than team because the leaders of a team balance one another. There is nothing, other than the skill of the Whip, to prevent a tandem leader from turning round and facing his driver. The weight of a team can often be too much for the average lady so a tandem provides the answer for those who have ambitions to handle four reins skilfully. Anyone who can drive a tandem competently could get up behind a well-trained team and drive them for a short distance in reasonable safety.

Handling tandem reins

Before sitting behind a tandem, it is wise to set up weights and pulleys (see Fig. 16b) as for single, so that the handling of the four reins can be thoroughly understood before it is attempted with the horses. It will be necessary to have four weights and four reins attached to four ropes over four pulleys. These must be assembled in such a way that the leader's reins come back to the hands on top of the wheeler's reins as they will with the live turn-out. The near leader's rein lies over the index finger of the left hand. The off leader's rein lies under the index finger. The near wheeler's rein lies under the off leader's rein and on top of the middle finger so that there are two reins lying together between these two fingers. The off wheeler's rein lies under the middle finger. The reins remain in this left hand and are *never* taken from this position. The right hand, which holds the whip at all times, is placed in front of the left and, for going straight, separates the left reins and the right reins with the middle and third fingers so that the nearside reins lie over the middle finger and both offside reins lie under the third finger. The simplest way to get these right-hand fingers into this position, when it is first attempted, is to place the right hand near the pulleys so that the left and right reins can be easily distinguished. The fingers are put into position, separating the left and right reins, and the right hand is then slid back until it lies just in front of the left hand with the index

72 *The handling of four reins in the left hand.*

73 *The right hand in position in front of the left, on four reins.*

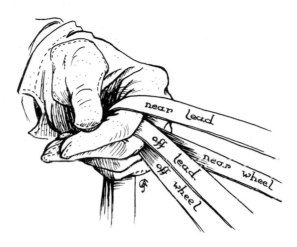

Fig. 26 *Holding reins for tandem and four-in-hand driving etc.*

finger on top of the near lead rein. An incline to the right can be made with both off-side reins being pressed down by the right hand at the same time as the left hand is turned, as with single and pair, to lengthen the left reins in general and the near leader in particular. A left incline is made by rotating the left hand, as with single and pair, to tighten the near leader and by increasing contact on the near leader and/or near wheeler with the middle finger of the right hand.

Practice with the weights and pulleys will reveal whether or not the correct pressure is being put onto the desired reins. It is very important to make sure that the weights are level before each incline is made so that the truth is seen and that errors can be rectified. Once these left and right inclines have been perfected, the more difficult sharp turns can be tried. There are various ways of executing sharp turns and much depends on the lightness and obedience of the horses. One successful method is, on the approach to a sharp left turn, to put opposition onto the off wheeler with the little or third finger of the right hand. This will incline the wheeler a little from the direction of the turn and hold him off the corner to prevent him from perhaps putting the left wheel in a ditch or the left hub against a gate post. As the leader approaches the turning to be made, he can be brought to the left by the left wrist being turned to put pressure onto the near lead rein. Should this not be enough, the middle finger of the right hand can reach and press the left rein. Once the leader has come round and the wheeler is clear of the corner hazard, he can be allowed to follow the leader.

163

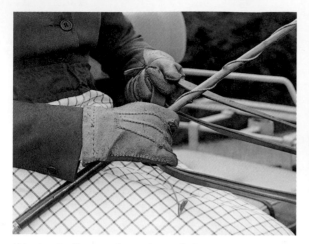 

74 *An incline to the right with four reins.*   75 *An incline to the left with four reins.*

When a sharp turn to the right is made, the near wheeler rein must be used to oppose the wheeler from the corner, with the middle finger of the right hand. Then the left hand should be turned to lengthen the near lead rein to allow the leader round as pressure is put onto the off lead rein by the third finger of the right hand to give the leader the office to turn right. As soon as the corner is clear then the wheeler can be allowed to follow. If the horses are less sensitive they may need stronger handling and a rein, on occasions, might have to be looped. In looping, a part of one rein is picked up with the right hand and placed under the thumb of the left hand. Once a loop has been made it is held by the thumb, which effectively gives the Whip the equivalent of a third hand. The fingers can be used, whilst the loop is kept, to hold whichever horse is concerned away from or into a turn as desired. The loop is released when it is no longer needed by raising the left thumb. It is less usual to use loops with a tandem than with a team when it is necessary owing to the sideways pull on coupling reins as with a pair. Also a team needs much stronger handling to keep the wheelers off corners. Tandems, in general, need much more delicate handling. Another way of making a tight turn with a tandem is to take the lead rein for the desired turn and the opposite wheel rein, simultaneously, which brings the leader round and holds the wheeler off the corner. A left turn can be executed in this way by putting pressure on the top and bottom reins and a right turn by taking more contact on the two central reins. These reins are used in this manner if the

164

76 *A loop in the near wheeler's rein.*

tandem is temporarily offset when it should be going straight. If the leader goes momentarily to the right and the wheeler goes to the left, a little pressure on the top and bottom reins, with the right hand, will straighten them immediately. Conversely, if they are offset with the leader to the left and the wheeler to the right then a little pressure on the two central reins, with the right hand, will straighten them.

Throughout all these manoeuvres, the left hand *never ever* moves from holding the reins in the initial 'coaching' position. The right hand is, at all times, held in front of the left, on the reins, ready to apply pressure on individual or pairs of reins as necessary. Tandem reins may be shortened or lengthened in exactly the same way as with single and pair driving but it is difficult, by that method, to shorten the reins substantially. Another method of shortening the reins is to use the right hand, behind the left hand, to secure the reins temporarily, as one, while the left hand is slid forward the required amount. On no account must the reins be shortened by the left hand being removed and the driver attempting to climb up the reins as if they were a rope.

All this needs to be practised with the weights and pulleys so that a system of handling which makes some kind of sense can be understood before sitting up behind the horses. Skilful handling requires considerable dexterity and it is not surprising that tandem driving has been compared with playing a harp.

Once the correct principles of rein handling have been established, then the individual Whip will develop his or her own techniques of fingering on the reins, as trained musicians do with their musical instruments. It is worth practising to establish the basic principles before developing unorthodox methods. Cross-country marathon driving often needs different methods of rein handling in order to cope with tight turns to negotiate obstacles when every second counts. However, if these unorthodox systems are practised too often before the

165

traditional coaching methods have been learnt, bad habits will develop which could be very hard to correct. Once the traditional method is learnt then there is no harm to be done by using different methods of rein handling when the need arises. For normal driving conditions, and for showing and dressage tests, the old established method is best if a consistently straight and steady tandem is to be produced.

Folding a tandem whip

Catching the thong of a tandem whip in the correct, traditional way is a skilled art and best practised on foot before any attempt is made to do this whilst driving the horses.

A tandem whip has a much longer thong than those which are used for either single or pair driving, so that the leader can be reached. A thong on a 14.2 hand tandem whip is about three hundred and sixty-six centimetres (twelve feet) long with the stick about one hundred and fifty-two centimetres (five feet) long. The thong has to be folded along the stick when it is not in use. The aim is to have a loop of thong hanging from the end of the whip and for the rest of the thong to be wound a few times round the stick, at the top, by the loop, and for it to be wound a few more times at the end, by the handle. The lash is secured under the thumb to prevent the whip from unfolding unintentionally. The wheeler can, if necessary, be encouraged with the loop which is hanging at the end of the whip. The thong has to be unfolded in order to reach the leader and folded up again after it has been used.

One method of learning how to catch a tandem thong is to draw a very large S on a wall and stand in front of it. The whip is held in the right hand with the lash secured under the thumb. The S is followed, with the point of the whip, starting at the bottom, left-hand side. The whip is swept to the right and then from right to left and upwards and then to the right to catch the swinging thong on the nodes in a deep

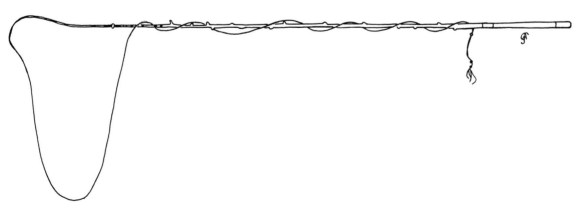

Fig. 27 *A folded tandem whip*

loop at the top of the stick with a few coils of thong around the stick and a small loop alongside the centre of the stick, and more coils, in the reverse direction, at the hand end. These coils near the hand have to be undone and turned in the opposite direction so that all the coils round the stick are going the same way, otherwise the thong will unfold immediately. To do this, the stick is brought down and held by the left hand, alongside the reins, whilst the right hand uncoils these turns and winds the thong and lash round the stick so that all the coils are going the same way.

It is necessary when choosing a tandem whip to find one which is not only light and well balanced but also has numerous little nodes at the top of the stick, in order that the thong can be caught and will be held in place by these protuberances. It is almost impossible to catch a thong on a whip which has a plain stick. Nylon whips, such as those used for lungeing, can never be folded in the traditional way.

Tandem harness

Leader bridle
The bridle which is used on a tandem leader is exactly the same as that used for a single turn-out.

Leader collar
The collar is the same as for a single whether it is a breast collar or a full collar. It is quite acceptable to use a breast collar on the leader and a full collar on the wheeler. If tandem bars are used, then single traces are long enough for the leader. If tandem bars are not used, then long lead traces are needed to reach back to the fittings on the wheeler's trace tug buckles. Tandem lead traces have spring cock-eyes at the ends to fasten them to the tug-buckle fittings. Some lead traces have a dee on the lower side to take a point strap for a false belly band. This point can be sewn to the dee or it can be made from a strap with a single keeper enabling it to be pulled through and held in place like a lip strap on a riding bridle.

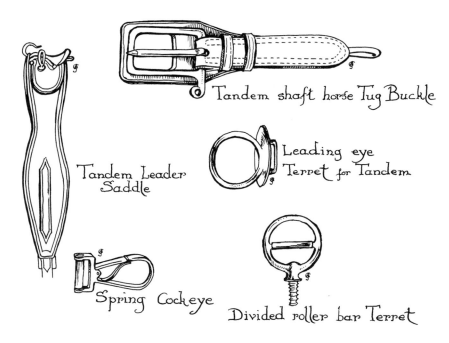

Tandem shaft horse Tug Buckle

Tandem Leader Saddle

Leading eye Terret for Tandem

Spring Cockeye

Divided roller bar Terret

Fig. 28 *Parts of tandem harness*

169

Leader saddle

The saddle for a tandem leader is similar in shape to that on a wheeler but it does not have a back band as there are no shaft tugs. There is, of course, no slot for a back band. There are loops at the sides of the panels through which the traces pass, to hold them up. The crupper and trace carrier should be of the martingale design so that there are no points of leather in which the leader's reins can get caught as this results in loss of steering. The trace carrier can be simply made, for a 14.2 animal, with a single strip of leather which is about one hundred and sixty-eight centimetres (five feet and six inches) long by about two centimetres (three quarters of an inch) in width. Of course, for show harness this would be made with two layers of leather which have been

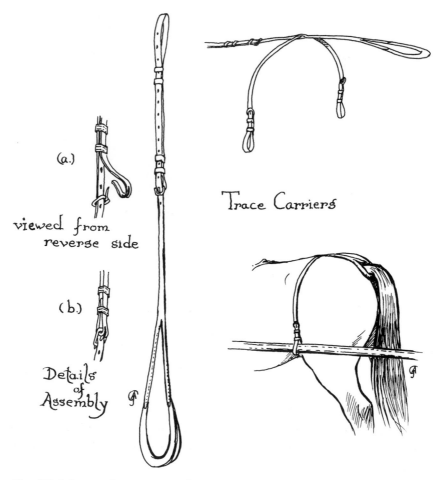

Fig. 29 *Martingale crupper and trace carriers*

77 *A tandem leader with the correct saddle, martingale type crupper and trace carrier and false belly band.*

sewn together. Also needed are two buckles which fit the width of the leather, and four well-fitting loose keepers. A long hole is cut in each end of the leather and three or four holes punched, for adjustment, with the first being put about twenty-three centimetres (nine inches) from the long hole. To assemble these pieces to make a trace carrier, the buckle is put onto the leather the correct way round, so that it lies in place in one of the holes. Next, the two loose keepers are threaded onto the strap and then a loop is made at this end of the strap and the leather passed up through the two keepers. The end now has to be taken right round the lower side of the buckle. To do this, the tongue of the buckle has to be removed from the hole into which it has just been put. The tongue can be passed through the long hole before being returned to the small, punched, hole. One keeper is pushed up to hold the buckle in place and the other keeper is pushed gently down to keep the loop to form one end of the trace carrier. The carrier can now be threaded through the slot in the crupper back strap and the same method that has just been described is employed at the other end, with the other buckle and two keepers, to make the trace carrier complete.

The martingale crupper is made and assembled in a similar way but using three or four loose keepers as well as one buckle. The crupper dock is stitched in place so that there are no points of leather which can catch the leader's reins.

Leader reins

The reins which are needed for the tandem leader are very long. Those of about eight hundred and twenty-three centimetres (twenty-seven feet) are right for a 14.2 tandem. Some people use webbing reins but these are not as easy or pleasant to handle as leather.

Wheeler bridle

The wheeler's bridle differs from the leader's in that rosettes with terrets, known as leading-eye terrets, are put onto each side of the brow band to take the leader's reins. Some people use either drop rings, or

Roger rings, on the throatlash, instead, as they give a more direct line to the leader. It is necessary to use a bit with a bar across the bottom to prevent the leader's reins from getting caught in the cheeks of the wheeler's bit.

78 *The wheeler's bridle with a bar Liverpool bit and leading eye terrets to take the leader's reins.*

Fig. 30 *Roger Ring*

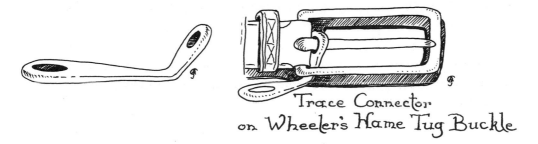

Trace Connector
on Wheeler's Hame Tug Buckle

Fig. 31 *Tandem trace connector*

Wheeler collar

Traditionally made tandem wheeler hame tug buckles have a protruberance on the lower sides to take the spring cock-eyes at the ends of the leader's traces. Nowadays, many people use a metal trace connector which is sometimes called a spoon. It has a hole at one end to take the cock-eye and another hole at the other end, which fits over the point of the hame tug buckle accentuating the need for this to be made of steel. A great deal of pressure is applied to the leather round the area where the connector is fixed to the tongue of the buckle. It is a good idea to protect this with either a loose strip of leather, which has a hole cut into it to enable it to lie under the connector and over the leather

79 *The wheeler's hame tug buckle with the brass plated steel connector taking the steel spring cock-eye on the leader's trace.*

173

where the tongue comes through, or to get a harness maker to cover this area with a piece of thin metal. Then, when the leader is put into draught and pressure is transmitted from the leader's traces onto the spoon, and in turn to the wheeler's hame tug buckle tongue, and through his traces to the trace hooks on the vehicle, no damage is done to the leather which fastens the wheeler's hame tug buckles to the hame tugs on the collar.

Wheeler saddle

It is necessary to have divided terrets on the wheeler's saddle for two reasons. One is that the roller bar keeps the leader's and wheeler's reins apart, preventing them from sticking together. The other is that if the reins run together through the terret, they can become reversed in position, with the leader's rein getting below the wheeler's, and this can be very confusing for a beginner in the art of handling four reins. For the sake of uniformity, it looks smart to have a martingale crupper to match that on the leader.

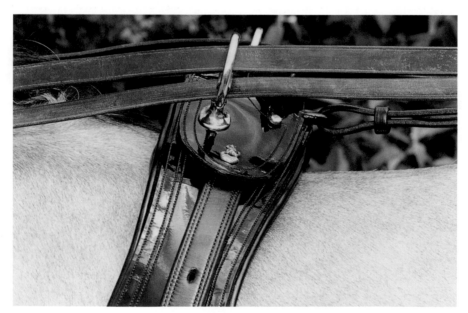

80 *The wheeler's saddle with the leader's reins lying through the upper half of the terrets and the wheeler's reins through the lower half.*

Wheeler reins

The same reins are used with a tandem wheeler as for a single turn-out.

174

Harnessing a tandem

Harnessing a tandem can be compared, in many ways, to harnessing two singles. The wheeler is harnessed in exactly the same way with, of course, all the additions previously mentioned. His reins are passed through the lower half of the divided terrets on his saddle and folded through the crupper back strap instead of through the terret because this would get in the way of the leader's reins when putting to.

Harnessing the tandem leader differs in some ways from harnessing a single, apart from the collar, which is put on first as usual, and the bridle which is the same. The saddle, crupper and trace carriers go on after the collar but there is no breeching. The long traces are buckled to the trace tugs and passed though the loops on the saddle and the loops on the trace carrier. They can now be put over the animal's back ready for putting to. If a false belly band is used, this can be buckled to the points coming down from the dees on the lower sides of the traces. If there are dees for these on the traces but no false belly band is used, ensure that the traces are put on the right way round so that the dees lie downwards.

Each rein is attached on its own side, so that each is folded through the saddle terret and secured with a quick release loop. As these reins are so long, care must be taken that each is secured firmly. The nearside rein is folded through the nearside terret and the offside rein is secured through the offside terret. This makes it easier when putting to. There is no buckle on the end of the reins, just a single keeper on one through which the point on the end of the other one is passed to hold them together. This is so that in an emergency the reins will slip apart and run through the wheeler's harness. It also makes taking out of the vehicle easier as there is no little buckle to be undone.

Tandem bars

Some people use tandem bars to connect the leader to the wheeler, in preference to long leader traces. They claim that the likelihood of getting a leader's hind leg or wheeler's front leg over a trace is lessened if bars are used. Single harness traces can be used for the leader, if bars are employed. The lead bar, for a 14.2 hand tandem, is about seventy-four centimetres (two feet and five inches) wide with a trace hook at each end. The wheeler bar is about fifty-eight centimetres (one foot eleven inches) wide. The two bars are connected at their centres by a long hook. There is a light strap attached to the under side, at the centre, of the wheeler bar which is passed through a slot at the end of the connecting hook and buckled back to a small buckle on the wheeler bar. Its purpose is to prevent the wheeler's bar bit from getting caught in the long hook and to prevent the leader's bar from jumping off. There is a ring at each end of the wheeler's bar, onto which a short length of trace, about fifty-three centimetres (one foot and nine inches), is sewn. Each has a spring cock-eye, at the end, which is hooked onto trace connectors on the wheeler's hame tug buckles. The wheeler's bar is fastened to his hame chain ring, or a ring on the lower hame strap, by a small spring hook on the end of about twenty-three centimetres (nine inches) of light chain. This prevents the bars from falling right down onto his front legs. Tandem bars are usually made from wood and are finished in paint or varnish to match that of the vehicle. The metal fittings are also made to match those on the carriage and harness.

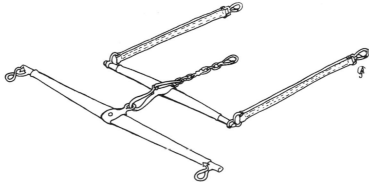

Fig 32. *Tandem bars*

Putting to a tandem

The wheeler is put to in exactly the same way as a single horse and is then held by a groom. If tandem bars are used, these are attached to the wheeler's hame tug buckles and lower hame strap or hame chain, after he has been put to.

The leader is led into position in front of the wheeler and held by a second groom. The golden rule of putting a tandem to is that the leader's reins must now be passed from the leader's saddle terrets through the wheeler's bridle terrets and through the upper half of the wheeler's saddle terrets. They do not pass through the hame or collar terrets but should be folded over the back strap ready to be picked up before mounting. The Whip should take the four reins in the correct position for driving, making sure that they are level, and can then mount. If there is only one groom then he can stand at either the leader's head or between the wheeler and the leader, in which case the lead reins are held level in one hand and the wheel reins held near the bit in the other hand. A glance at the nearest splices on the leader's reins will show if they are being held evenly.

When the Whip has settled on the box, with whip in hand and his rug over his knees and has control over both horses, the leader's traces can be attached. Similar systems are used whether tandem bars or long traces are employed. The difference between the two systems is that long traces are fixed to the wheeler's hame tug buckles by spring cock-eyes whereas, with tandem bars, the leader's traces are fixed to the lead bar by their crew holes. The offside lead trace can be fastened first and the nearside trace can be hooked into place. When the Whip is ready to move off the groom can mount. This is one of the safest methods of putting to because it ensures that the leader's traces are not hooked onto the wheeler until the last moment before moving off. *Never ever* put the traces on, from the leader to the wheeler, before running the reins through from the leader to the wheeler. If anything should frighten the leader he will be likely to take off, pulling the wheeler and carriage away in the process and there will be nothing that anyone is able to do. Certainly, pulling on the wheeler's reins will have little effect if he and the carriage are being dragged along by a terrified leader.

On returning home from a drive, the safest method of taking the animals out is for the groom to dismount and for the Whip to stay on the box. The leader's traces are unhooked from the wheeler. The leader's reins are then carefully pulled through from the Whip's hands and through the wheeler's saddle terrets and bridle terrets. Great care must be taken as it has been known for a wheeler's bridle to be pulled off by a careless groom who was trying to hurry. The leader's reins are folded through his saddle terrets on each side. The Whip can now dismount, as for a single, and take the wheeler from the vehicle.

If a groom should, for some reason, be left to hold both horses, the only safe way for him to do this is to stand alongside the wheeler's head with his reins in one hand and the leader's reins in the other hand. It is no use for a groom to stand at the leader's head if he has to control both animals. The wheeler can go wherever he likes, with the carriage, and is almost certain to drag the leader with him. Equally, trying to hold the wheeler without control over the leader will be of no use in a crisis. The real answer is to lessen the problem by unhooking the leader's traces if one person has to hold both animals for more than a few seconds.

Driving a tandem

It is essential to have a whip which is long enough to enable the leader to be reached. A light lungeing whip is adequate for everyday or cross-country use when an expensive holly whip might get broken. The main disadvantage of a nylon whip is that the thong cannot be folded correctly. It has to be wound a few times round the stick and then held in place in the right hand. The thong is unwound if it is needed to encourage the leader; a loop of thong can be used on the wheeler if necessary. A good way of retrieving the thong after it has been used on the leader is to swing it back and catch it between the upper arm and the body. This is much easier than trying to catch it with the right hand which, because it is also holding the stick, may have to make several abortive attempts before the lash is finally caught.

There are two common causes of accidents with a tandem. One is the failure by the Whip to oppose the shaft horse during a tight turn, which can result in the inside wheel being run up a bank, so causing a capsize. The other most common cause is failure on the part of the Whip to notice that the lead reins are being gently but steadily pulled out of the left hand by an onward going leader. The leader's traces tighten and the draught goes right through the wheeler's traces to the trace hooks on the vehicle. Novice drivers tend to think that their shaft horse is being lazy when, in fact, he is probably being almost pulled off his feet. His collar is being dragged up his neck and his breeching is tightened as the leader gets more and more in draught. Hitting the wheeler forward is not always the answer. The instant cure is to shorten the lead reins by about twenty-three centimetres (nine inches) or more. The lead traces will instantly slacken and the wheeler can then be sent into his collar and made to pull the vehicle. So the two main things to remember are: opposing the wheeler before a sharp corner and keeping the leader out of draught unless the intention is to have him working *as well* as the shaft horse.

The only time that the leader of a private driving tandem turn-out should be in draught is when the wheeler needs help to pull the load up a steep hill or when the going is deep or muddy. Other than that, the lead traces should always hang with a little slack between the leader and the wheeler. The steering becomes lost if the leader is in draught

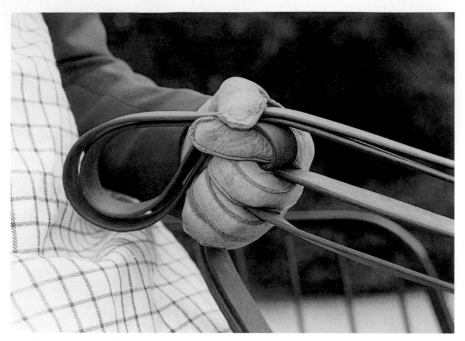

81 *Loops in both lead reins.*

round corners. If the leader gets into draught when going down a hill, the wheeler is very likely to be pulled onto his knees. When descending a hill, the easiest way to keep the leader out of draught is to take loops in both lead reins. The loops are held under the left thumb and the leader is kept back by whatever amount of rein, say fifteen centimetres (six inches), is being held by the thumb. The right hand is then free to help the left with the steadying and steering. If, on descending a steep hill, a sharp turn has to be made, the loops keep the leader out of draught whilst the right hand is free to put pressure on whichever reins are needed to complete the turn. When the bottom of the hill is reached, the left thumb can be carefully raised to release the loops slowly and the leader will go forward to take up the slack traces. It is essential to keep an eye on the lead traces all the time. They must be seen to swing very slightly. They must not be too loose. It is easy to get either a wheeler's front leg or a leader's hind leg over a trace which is too slack.

A watch should be kept on the wheeler's breeching. If this is tight, when going on the level, or worse still, up a hill, then the leader is in too much draught and pulling the wheeler along. A tug of war is being created.

It is for this reason that, when moving off, it is important to ensure that either the wheeler steps forward fractionally before the leader, or that they go forward as one. Before moving off it is essential to see that the lead traces are hanging correctly in a slight loop. If the leader goes forward before the wheeler, difficulties are always created. The leader comes up against a dead pull which probably causes him to stop or hesitate. As he stops, the slower thinking wheeler steps forward. He may even push the shaft tip into the leader's hindquarters or step on the leader's heels, which causes the sharper thinking leader to leap forward. The result can be imagined.

The beginner to tandem driving will probably discover all these things for himself. A great deal can be learnt from sitting alongside an expert and watching how he handles the four reins. If the offer to drive arises, then it is sensible to take the opportunity to have a go whilst the expert is there to help. It can be discouraging to see the straight, onward going tandem immediately transform into a crooked wandering pair within moments of the reins being transferred. However, the satisfaction when things go right is worth every bit of the misery when everything seems to go wrong.

More multiples

Once pair and tandem driving have been mastered, there is natural progression to driving three horses. Often a spare horse which matches the two may have been found and it is understandable that thoughts should then turn to random (three in a row), unicorn (two wheelers and one leader) or trandem (three abreast).

Harness for random can be made up with a set of tandem wheeler harness for the shaft horse and both sides of the set of pair harness for the leader and swing (centre) horse. Two pairs of long tandem leader traces are needed. A second pair of divided terrets is wanted for the swing horse, as is another pair of bridle terrets. The greatest expense is the long reins which are essential to reach the leader. The tandem lead and wheel reins are used for the swing and shaft horses. All that applies to tandem driving also applies to random driving. The reins are secured in the left hand. The near lead goes over the index finger, off lead under the index finger, near swing under the off lead, off swing under the middle finger. The near wheel goes over the third finger and the off wheel under the third finger. Handling is similar to tandem as far as both hands are concerned. The important thing to watch is the traces and on no account must the leader or swing horse get into draught more than the shaft horse or they will pull him off his feet. Obviously, for this form of driving, it is essential to have onward going and sensible animals who have good mouths.

Unicorn harness can be made up with either team-wheeler harness or the pair harness with an additional central terret to take the leader's reins. The leader can wear one side of a set of pair harness or tandem leader harness with team lead traces which have cock-eyes to go onto the lead bar which is fixed to the crab on the pole head. The leader's reins are taken through the leading eye terrets on the inner sides of the wheeler's bridles.

Trandem, three abreast, can be put to in all kinds of ways. One way is with three sides of pair harness. Two poles and four pole straps are used with a widened splinter bar, having six roller bolts, on a four-wheeled carriage. Two draught reins go to the hands with two lots of coupling reins from each so that when one rein is pulled, all three

82 *Araminta Winn driving Mr and Mrs Mike Underwood's champion Welsh Section A ponies in unicorn to a four-wheeled Ralli Car at the British Driving Society Show at Smith's Lawn, Windsor.*

horses are brought round. Obviously, the adjustment of the coupling reins is critical if all three animals are able to work evenly.

Another way of driving three abreast can be with a single between the shafts of a two-wheeled vehicle and one animal in specially devised harness on each side. Traces are hooked to swingle trees attached to the front of the vehicle enabling all three to pull together. Breechings work on all three as the outer animal's harness is fixed to the shaft ends. As the vehicle runs forward, so all the animals take the weight on their quarters.

Once three horses have been put together, it is a short step to putting in a team. All that has been said about rein handling of tandems and coupling of pairs applies to a four in hand. When driving there is more weight in the hands and the looping of reins is usually necessary for turns.

The golden rule when putting multiples to their carriages *is always* to run the reins through the terrets so that horses can be controlled by the

83 A trandem in New Zealand, owned and driven by Jack Field.

Whip and grooms before any traces are ever hooked onto trace attachments to the carriage.

Multiples of sixes, eights, tens and so on, up to the famous forty-horse hitch, which is seen in Milwaukee, USA, are harnessed and driven.

If rein handling is taken seriously and practised correctly with a single, who knows what the future may hold for the newcomer to the art of driving a harness horse.

Index

Page numbers in *italics* refer to illustrations